Defying '

Dr. Eric Shannon Parr

Defying the Lies: A Memoir

Dr. Eric Shannon Parr

Defying the Lies: A Memoir

Dr. Eric Shannon Parr

Dr. Eric Shannon Parr

Defying the Lies: A Memoir, June 2023, Second Edition
Copyright 2023 by Dr. Eric Shannon Parr
ISBN: 979-8782171933 (eBook)
ISBN: 979-8378299317 (Paperback)
ISBN: 979-8378601141 (Hardcover)
All rights reserved.

First edition of Defying the Lies: A Memoir, previously entitled Defying the Lies, published November 2020.
ISBN: 979-8680749425 (Paperback)

Book design by Dr. Eric Shannon Parr.
Pictures and illustrations by Dr. Eric Shannon Parr.
Edited by Dr. Eric Shannon Parr.
Cover art designed and created by Dr. Eric Shannon Parr.

For booking inquiries:
DrEricShannonparrEdD@gmail.com

Dr. Eric Shannon Parr

The information and photography presented in this book are a representation of the views, perspectives, and experiences of incidents and scenarios that occurred throughout Dr. Eric Shannon Parr's lifetime as of the date of this publication. This book is presented for information and entertainment purposes only. Due to the rate at which things change, the author reserves the right to alter, modify, or update the information presented in this book based on new conditions.

While every attempt has been made to verify the content of this book, neither the author nor his affiliates or partners assume any responsibility for errors, inaccuracies, or omissions. Names, specific dates, and times may have been omitted, altered, or changed to preserve the continuity, secrecy, or confidentiality of the content of this book. Reference to event times and information in retrospect to particular situations, events, and scenarios within this book is provided with the readers' assumed understanding that information contained herein, including facts, references, and reflections, may be given in hindsight.

All photographs, pictures, and written content contained within this book are the sole property of, copyrighted, and protected by Dr. Eric Shannon Parr. No reproductions, depictions of photographs, pictures, or written content contained in this book may be copied, shared, or duplicated without the sole written permission from Dr. Eric Shannon Parr. Neither the whole nor any part of this book may be sold or reproduced in any form by any electronic, manual, or mechanical means, including information storage and retrieval systems, without the expressed, written permission of Dr. Eric Shannon Parr.

For Rebecca

TABLE OF CONTENTS

Chapter 1	WAITING TO DIE	1
Chapter 2	GYPSY MOVERS	7
Chapter 3	MOTORCYCLE	15
Chapter 4	HOPE	25
Chapter 5	FIRST GRADE LLAMA	31
Chapter 6	SNAKES	35
Chapter 7	BLACK DEATH	41
Chapter 8	FOOTBALL FREAK	47
Chapter 9	ACTING THE PART	55
Chapter 10	FUN NAVY TORTURE	63
Chapter 11	NAVY SCHOLAR	81
Chapter 12	SCIENTIFIC SQUADRON	91

Chapter 13	CHEATING DEATH	101
Chapter 14	SURVIVE OR DIE	109
Chapter 15	MONSTER ICE TRUCK	125
Chapter 16	PLACE IN THIS WORLD	133
Chapter 17	TRAGIC LEGACY	137
Chapter 18	INVENTION	149
Chapter 19	JONAH EXPERIENCE	153
Chapter 20	BUILDING A BUSINESS	165
Chapter 21	OLD COLLEGE TRY; AGAIN	169
Chapter 22	KIDNEY PUNCTURE NEEDLES	175
Chapter 23	COLLEGE CONTINUED	189
Chapter 24	DEFYING THE PAIN	195
Chapter 25	DOCTORATE PURSUIT	205
Chapter 26	MY SUPERHERO HAS CANCER	209
Chapter 27	SIGNS OF LIFE	217
Chapter 28	KIDNEY DIALYSIS LIFE	229

Chapter 29	UNEXPLAINABLE SURGERY 239
Chapter 30	DIALYSIS REALITY 251
Chapter 31	DOCTORATE COMEBACK 261
Chapter 32	GIFT OF LIFE 267
Chapter 33	RECORDS BROKEN 281
Chapter 34	ACADEMIC FINISH LINE 285
Chapter 35	THE JOURNEY CONTINUES 291

Chapter 1:

WAITING TO DIE

Missouri is known for having some crazy weather. One day it could be thirty degrees and snowing, then seventy-five and a cloudless blue sky the next. This particular day, it was a balmy eighty-five degrees with puffy white clouds dotting the southern sky.

I loved the changes and unexpected feelings of having several different seasons in January. But this southwest winter day was not the norm, feeling the warm breeze as frosty air permeated my clothes, leaving me with a feeling of winter all around. Even my feet were cold. It was weird to say the least.

Returning from the gym that evening, I went inside my apartment, turned up the thermostat to eighty, and made a pot of caffeinated goodness. Standing in front of the brewing fresh pot of coffee, I was puzzled by how ridiculously cold I was, not figuring out what was going on here. I mean, c'mon! I had been to Antarctica, the coldest place on planet Earth, surviving one hundred and twenty degrees below zero wind chills.

Thinking I could warm up from the now continuous bone-knocking chills shooting in steady waves throughout my body, I climbed into my bed. Nope. They were so bad that my bed frame shook. I did not want to admit it, but something was very wrong. Due to Brotherly "disagreements," we had not talked for a while, but I had to let him know what happened. I made a phone call that night to my brother and told him how I felt.

Without any hesitation, he told me to get to the hospital immediately. Being the big brother who thought he knew more than he did, I thought I could tough it out. Besides, I did not want to act out of fear. If it became worse, I could pray to see if there was something later I needed to do.

I jumped out of bed and went to the bathroom, threw open the shower curtain, and cranked on the water to scalding. Waiting for it to warm up, I saw goosebumps appear on my arms when the cold air mixed with the steam coming from the hot water. I jumped into that warm, watery escape, and as soon as that first shot of hot water hit my skin, my entire body shuddered.

The stark difference between the chill of my skin and the water temperature shocked my system like lightning. Every part of my body turned a dark shade of red the longer I stayed under the water, but I did not care. If second-degree burns were the result, so be it.

I repeated this insane water routine several times, remaining motionless until the water ran cold. But no matter how many times I climbed back into the shower, I could not get rid of those freaking chills. These secretive enemies of warmth crept down into the very core of my being, popping back up with an unrelenting vengeance. The water routine was not working, so I put on several layers of clothes. I made some more coffee, gulped it down, turned my apartment heater up some more, and jumped into bed. Pulling the covers over my head to make a heat seal, I soon realized this was a really bad idea. A puddle of sweat started developing under my body from the heat, growing larger and larger.

The longer I stayed under the layers of covers and sheets, the colder I became. My clothes began sticking to my body like I had them glued onto me. Feeling as if I was in some sort of freezing water sauna, my body racked with uncontrollable trembling. Then I started to itch, and man, it was awful.

This was not a nagging summer mosquito bite. No, sir, it was far beyond it, similar to a ravenous poison ivy irritation my brother suffered in first grade, just after he broke his arm. No matter how much he tried using a coat hanger to relieve the itch from the inflamed rash inside his cast, it only worsened from sweating. And when I scratched, the spot also seemed to move.

Over the next several hours, the relentless itching developed into a burning irritation. As much as I tried to ease the suffering, it would not be relieved, coming from deep under my skin. I thought if I scratched deep enough, I could stop this torture, but to no avail.

Sometimes you have to face the fact that nothing else can be done about a situation, no matter how much you try to defeat the enemy of your sanity. I truly believed I could overcome this thing, rationalizing all of it despite the apparent, making my mind accept this unholy torture. I had eventually overcome worse in other life situations, so why not this?

After what felt like several hours, not being able to sleep for obvious reasons, I called a friend. Trying to tell her everything I had been experiencing over the last several hours was difficult because my head was now in a thick fog, everything around me melting into a dull haze. She kept telling me to repeat my words because I was now having trouble talking. After a few minutes of hearing my incoherent blabbering, she flat-out said to get my butt to the hospital. She was always one to tell it like it is and never pulled any punches with me.

By now, I was completely out of it, rambling and staggering around the apartment. She talked me through finding my clothes, wallet, and eventually leaving my place. Good God, if she were not on the other end of the line, something very bad might have happened.

Miraculously, I drove to the hospital because no one was available. When I walked through the hospital's sliding glass doors, the nurse at the front desk asked what was wrong with me and who drove me there. They were shocked when I said "nobody," presumably because of how I looked, and now I can barely speak.

By now, delirium set in, and I started mumbling out loud, looking around at the ceiling and the people in the emergency room waiting area. A nurse urgently ran around from behind the intake desk and helped me to sit down, took my vitals, and then rushed off. What seemed like only a few minutes, a gurney rushed up beside me, and the man pushing said, "Get on now." Helping me climb up, he quickly pushed through a set of large wooden, swinging doors to the right of the emergency room and down a long corridor where people and families were packed in tightly, gurneys and chairs end to end on either side of the hall.

A blurry mass of people with bleeding legs, gaping cuts, superficial scrapes, broken bones, and all kinds of bad injuries followed me with their eyes, probably wondering what I was doing being whisked past so fast. He wheeled me into a private room full of machines, screens, monitors, and plastic bags with intravenous tubes hanging on racks. Nurses quickly came in after I was helped onto the bed and put needles into my arms, hooking me up to machines and bags, starting fluids in my veins, and taking lots of blood.

     Doctors rushed in and out of my room, repeatedly checking my vitals, trying to figure out what was wrong with me. Come to find out, my body's systems were shutting down because my blood was thick as sludge, toxic, and full of poisons. Blood nitrogen levels were ten times the body's normal range, indicated by the extreme itching and delirium. Barely hearing the blips, bleeps, and fluttering sounds from the machinery reflecting my heartbeat, oxygen levels, and blood pressure, I felt as if my spirit could leave my body at any moment. I was dying.

Defying the Lies: A Memoir

Chapter 2:

GYPSY MOVERS

Before my seventh birthday, I became a professional traveler. We moved eight times, going from state to state, school to school, and environment to environment. These constant transitions did not include going from one house to another, to a farm out in the middle of nowhere, or

from apartments to condominiums.

If ever there was a way to stop the constant shifting madness, I would have raised my little hand and asked not to be exposed to the extreme, repeated changes, eventually triggering emotional and psychological issues later in life. Yes, it was the 1970s when kids were more independent, but lacking parental structure in terms of emotional consideration was not the norm in my household.

Shortly after I was born, we moved from Louisiana to Florida. Dad found us a small ranch-style apartment with a state-of-the-art window air conditioning unit. Our place was set right off the main road, leading to the beach that was just down the road and across the street. As soon as we moved into the little place, Mom started setting up her house, complete with green vinyl chairs, yellow lamps, and brown coffee tables.

Years later, she told me it was so nice to have a place to decorate in classic 1970s style, insisting on a nice, safe space she could call her own, and stability for her children.

I was a curious little guy who was very energetic and never stopped moving, constantly exploring our new house, and getting into whatever was around. My favorite toys were Mom's pots and pans. Every time I crawled over to her pantry, Mom took out different sizes of her favorite stainless-steel cookware. I loved banging on my pretend drum set, babbling my songs out loud while she happily sang along, laughing and cooking next to me.

Whenever she could, Mom took me to the beach to crawl on the cushy, warm sand. Picking out a nice, soft spot near the edge of the water, she made sure her umbrella, chair, and cooler filled with refreshments were properly placed, gingerly set me down, and watched me start exploring my amazing world at the ocean's edge.

I discovered many types of colored sea shells and little soft-shell crabs, trying to go into the water more than once when the waves licked at my feet. The beach and old wooden dock, surrounded by old sailboats and fishing vessels, is where I loved to hang out. It was amazing, taking in the salty air and loving life as a little one.

    Mom nick-named me "Carrot Top" because my hair was so red it looked bright orange. I had fair skin and all the freckles on my nose and face that went with it. She made sure to protect me from sunburn in the bright Florida sun, slathering me up with thick white sunscreen. Nothing was going to happen to her little one.

    I think I would have enjoyed growing up in sunny, beautiful Florida, but Dad had other plans. Within a year of having made a life there, Dad found other kinds of electrical work back where I started this whole moving adventure. We packed up our stuff in the large orange and white moving van with the big tires, and away we went back to the unfriendly humidity and familiar atmosphere of Louisiana.

    We slowly but surely made our way up and across the United States. Mom and Dad took turns driving the family car behind the van. The trip took us three long days and nights, often stopping for rest in hotels, eating, using the bathroom, and filling up at the gas station.

    When we finally made it to Louisiana, we stayed with relatives until Dad found us a little apartment. Eventually, after living in a few temporary places, Dad decided it was finally time for us to settle down like an authentic, good old-fashioned American family.

    Dad saved enough money to build us a red brick house with all the trimmings, including a long, wide driveway, white shutters cupping large front windows, wooden flower trays, and a green lawn that looked like a big, beautiful emerald carpet. A fence surrounding the back of the property kept my brother and me safe while we played with neighborhood friends. Dad had the house built for 23,000 dollars, about 154,000 dollars in today's money. Not a small investment to be sure. He was very proud of this house designed for his young family.

After the house was built, mom and dad connected with other people in the neighborhood, developing friendships. It was fun to have our place. Mom had her Tupperware, dinner, and holiday parties. I watched dad cut the grass, and on several occasions, letting me try to help out, laughing and saying, "Maybe next time."

The edger fascinated and scared me at the same time, so I never went near that thing. We even bought a dog, but later found out the Husky had been abused as a puppy. Because of this, she was extremely mean, so we had to give her away.

Over the next few years, I had a lot of fun playing, living, and growing in that brick house. My three best friends, who were brothers, lived right next door. My little brother and I were close and shared the same friends. We enjoyed celebrating birthdays, yard parties, sliding down homemade water slides, and playing in sprinklers during the summer. Drinking out of the hose was even a given in the hot Louisiana summer.

Racing across the front driveway with my solid steel roller skates at full speed, I often injured myself because I only wore socks. Yeah, pretty stupid, but I thought I was tough. My parents thought stubbing my toes on the coarse concrete was punishment enough for rarely wearing my shoes, so they let me learn the hard way. I never really did.

My head was harder than they thought. I repeatedly skinned my toes and feet, but I did not care. The very next day, after injuring myself, I grabbed my skates, put on socks with bleeding feet, and ran outside right after breakfast to do it all over again. Part defiance and part boy, I just knew I was completely indestructible.

Since all of my extended family lived in Louisiana, we visited them as much as we could, especially on holidays, special occasions, and family reunions when Dad was not working, with cooking always being involved. The cooks in my family were unbelievable. From homemade pastries to freshly boiled seafood, every man and woman generations back could make anything incredible in the kitchen. To this day, I remember the taste of the pecan and pumpkin pie.

Every holiday, we took turns meeting at one another's homes for meals and visiting, with everyone pitching in to create unbelievable food. Smelling the deliciousness, we rushed in to see what was cooking in the large cast iron pots, bubbling up and creating hisses and pops of all the amazing dishes. It was a game to see who could run inside and grab a piece of pie, handfuls of cookies, or the most fingers dipped in dessert. It was always a feast with everyone pitching in on the cooking, and an amazing time to see each other.

My favorite of all the food served was my great-great-grandmother's chicken and dumplings, passed down through the generations. Whenever my Grandma mixed, kneaded, cut, and cooked long dumpling ribbons half an inch thick and almost a foot long, I always made sure I was the closest to the stove to get a taste of them first. So many of my relatives cooked amazingly, it was like having the pick of the best restaurants in her green and yellow vinyl kitchen. Pumpkin pies, pecan cookies, carrot cake, and every kind of confection you could imagine were at every gathering. Birthday parties always had a homemade bunny cake, Andy Boy cupcakes, or whatever the child wanted, custom-made to order.

One of the traditional Cajun dishes loved by all was boiled crawfish. There were usually hundreds of pounds of jumbo crawfish cooked in huge pots of seasoned boiling water until they became a deep reddish color, coated with more spicy seasonings, then dumped on a long row of tables strewn together. They were served with potatoes, corn on the cob, dipping sauce, and Louisiana Hot Sauce. We sat on either side with beer for the grownups and soda for the kiddos and went to town. Laughing and telling stories, we had a ball.

It was quickly eaten by my large family of cousins, aunts, uncles, nephews, nieces, grandmas, and grandpas, a voracity of hunger that rivaled a killer shark. Even the Cajun kids from ages two through the teenage years knew how it was done. We broke open the heads of the crawfish, sucked out the fat, peeled and ate the tail meat all in one movement, like old veteran Cajun seafood eaters.

My favorite aunt and uncle made the best Cush Cush every time I stayed over with them. They made it using homemade cornbread cut into thick slices. Then it was carefully put into a bowl with ice-cold milk, and a large spoonful of sugar was poured over it. Heated up or cold, it did not matter because I always looked forward to eating this amazing concoction when I went to their house.

Another thing I ate at their house was homemade pizza. When I say it was homemade, every single part of it, from the crust to the sauce, was handmade and homegrown. I am still convinced that the deliciousness would rival any modern pizza shop of today.

Pepperoni, anchovies, green peppers, sweet, mild, or spicy sauces, shredded cheeses of all kinds, fresh garden vegetables, pineapple and Hawaiian sausage, dried tomatoes, artichokes, and anything else you could imagine covered the seasoned dough. I loved making pizzas with them. Every time was an adventure, and every taste a new experience.

Many of my relatives lived near the swamps and backlands of Louisiana, and they were our Cajun playgrounds. When I was a little older, we went four-wheeling through the water and woods looking for snakes and turtles. We also went on adventures to the cold, muddy swamps for camping over the weekend to catch bullfrogs. At night, the grownups took a sharp dagger with three sharp points on the end of it called a Trident, similar to the one I used to kill snakes in our yard on the farm. They also grabbed nets and a flashlight, slowly trolling the shorelines while hanging over the front of a shallow boat seeking out the green croaking critters.

After enough frogs were caught, they were gutted, their legs were cut off, and then washed. Then, right there in the swamp camp, a large fire was made, and a huge cast-iron pot with cooking grease was placed on top, right in the middle. The battered frog legs and homemade hush puppies made from seasoned dough, jalapeños, and other secret ingredients were deep fried by lantern light to golden brown and eaten by the fire.

Another fun pastime was when we went sturgeon fishing on the shores of the Columbia River. People from all over came to try their luck. Men, women, and children old enough to do it hooked gigantic pieces of raw chicken onto the ends of large multi-pointed hooks tied onto thick fishing line with heavy weights. The raw bait was cast far from the shore into the waters with gigantic fishing poles made from either graphite or bamboo.

It became so crowded on the buzzing sandy shores that Dad had to constantly yell out over the noise to me and my brother, telling us to stay close. Getting stuck by the sharp barbs from the very large hooks that many people were casting was a common occurrence, so kids had to be aware. It was an unbelievable sight watching people sweat, curse, and barely reel in those giant sturgeon, getting up to sixteen feet long. As all of this was happening, I slowly walked in between the holes dug out for the fish in the soft, grainy ground, staring in amazement at these prehistoric bony-backed fish swishing their long tails.

Sharing these amazing adventures with family, living in our own house, and growing up with my best friends in our happy neighborhood only lasted a few short years until Dad caught wind of another electrical job opportunity. Mom, my brother, and I reluctantly uprooted our settled and familiar life, taking off across the United States to a dreary state of constant rain, strange wooden lands, colorfully wild mushrooms, and six-foot snow drifts. It took us almost a full week to travel from Louisiana to Oregon, a trip we would take multiple times as Dad constantly looked for the next best money-making opportunity.

Chapter 3:

MOTORCYCLE

I developed really bad anxiety and a dreadful fear of the unknown starting from a very young age. I did not know what would happen next from day to day, what type of people I would meet to have friends, or where we would end up next, because of constantly moving year to year. I knew I needed to have some kind of stability, but whenever I started a new school, I was always careful not to get attached to anyone or develop any friends because my life often shifted and changed. I became hyper sensitive to anything that shifted or moved around me, making me nervous and scared. Mom tried to console me whenever I felt mixed up or afraid, but it rarely helped. I was also nervous all the time, and my stomach hurt constantly.

    My parents took me to the doctor a few times, and I had to drink this chalky pink stuff to take a picture of my insides. Nothing was ever found, and the pain was a mystery to the doctors. Lining up my play cars in long rows helped me to cope a little bit, thinking that if I could keep my immediate world in order and things the way I wanted them, I might be okay. To this day, I have to make sure all of my things are organized and put in their proper place. The military training later in life only reinforced this obsessive practice.

Being an extremely emotional and impressionable child, I also took to heart whatever was said or done around me, making it a part of my identity. When I started to become angry, I hid my feelings by faking a smile, trying to be happy. Holding in all of these bad emotions caused restlessness, thinking that at any given moment, my world would be ripped apart yet again.

I fought daily thoughts of accepting this was my little life, not wanting it yet, having to do what Dad said. Like a good supportive wife in spite of her feelings, Mom went along with his every idea and quest for finding yet another location that might hold a better opportunity. She was very strong in not being obvious about her disappointment in dad while trying to console my mental anguish.

We relocated yet again when Dad started working at another company, this time for a big corporation. Every time we moved. I shoved my disappointment deeper down. This spawned an immense passive-aggressive, rebellious attitude against anything safe. I acted out my anger and resentment by doing crazy bike wheelies down remote streets, through ditches filled with muddy water, and busy streets of the neighborhood. I jumped ditches at full speed, and sometimes did other stupid stuff.

As a seven-year-old, I felt nothing could stop me on

my bicycle. After hopping off the side of my bike and slamming it onto the ground, I walked around it, grabbed it, and pedaled away to do it again and again. Mud puddles were no match for me, jumping headfirst into them, pounding my chest with a dirt-encrusted face.

I dared myself to do things that older kids would not try, like jumping over several people with a board leaning on top of tires in the middle of the street. Not knowing or understanding how to deal with feelings of contempt for ever-changing circumstances, I sought the rush of adrenaline to ignore my feelings. Soon, this rush appeared as metal, tires, and the smell of gasoline.

Dad had a friend he met through work who rode motocross. He and his wife invited my family to go see him race at the dirt race track. Sunday morning, Mom packed up some lunches and drinks, and we headed to see our first dirt bike races.

As we walked through the gigantic opening to the racetrack, I heard the roaring of high-pitched engines. I sat down and watched these loud machines called motorcycles speeding around the circular track. They were quickly jumping, skidding, and sometimes wrecking into the hay bales, each other, and tires lining the outside of the track. From that moment on, I was hooked. The motorcycles flying through the air mesmerized yet calmed me from the inside out.

Every time we went to the races, I just stared at the loud motorcycles, dreaming of jumping the big dirt track hills. The smell of gasoline pouring out of the bikes when

Defying the Lies: A Memoir

they were refueled or wrecked, the dust in the air, and excitement from the crowds so thick you could feel it around you like a blanket, was pure bliss. Even if they wore padding, people were injured during crashes and very badly sometimes, often hitting each other and sometimes people in crowds. Nevertheless, it never distracted me from watching wide-eyed with a big grin on my face.

Daydreaming at the track, I saw myself sitting on my motorcycle, revving up the engine with gears straining and whining. Taking off from the starting line, I would jump over the dirt hills. Passing through the last corner berms, I always crossed the finish line in first place.

During halftime, Dad let me take my little bicycle and pedal around the track, jumping the dirt hills and landing in the soft, sandy ground below. I was the only kid who went out there, and I did not care one bit. This was my new playground, and I wanted to have fun like the grown-ups.

After we went to the track one afternoon, I came home and begged my dad for a motorcycle at six years old. I asked him for several weeks until one day he had had enough and brought me to the speed shop in town. In the back was parked a used XR75 Honda with chrome spoke wheels, red tank, and a black seat.

As soon as I saw that beautiful machine, I fell in love. The kicker was that Dad had to buy it later because he simply did not have all of the money at that time. I hated knowing that I needed to wait even longer for my wish of rubber knobby tires and chrome spoke wheels to come true.

Every single day, I asked Dad when he was going to buy my dream machine. I became so restless, so utterly anxious that my stomach would burn and hurt. I never ate and was upset all the time, wanting to have my dream come true.

After several months of waiting, I eventually gave up. I tried to put off my feelings of disappointment by playing with Lincoln Logs, Lego sets, or riding my Big Wheel. In the best way I knew, I stuffed my feelings to not feel anything at all, and no one knew better. I pretended to be happy at home, but I never was. I guess my dream of having a motorcycle was just that, a dream.

One Monday afternoon, as every day before, I shuffled home with my head down from the neighborhood bus stop. Mom asked how my day went, gave me Cheetos and an oatmeal pie, and told me to sit at the kitchen table to eat it. Oddly enough, Dad was home. He walked into the room and also asked how I was, but I ignored him. He was working on something in the kitchen and told me in a weirdly-happy yet stern voice to go to the garage and get a wrench for him that was sitting on the steps.

Reluctantly, I walked to the garage door and heard chuckling from mom and dad. Opening the door, I froze in silence. Sitting in the middle of the garage with a bright red gas tank, black seat, silver shocks, and black knobby tires with chrome mag spoke rims was an XR75 Honda motorbike.

I could not believe it. My deepest heart's desire right there in front of me! I was in shock, slowly walking around it wide-eyed, running my hands over every shiny

Defying the Lies: A Memoir

part, bolt, bend, and bar that gleamed, sparkled, and glowed. I ran back into the kitchen and hugged Dad with everything in me, thanking him for my motorcycle. I was now the proud owner of a real-life Big Wheel destroying motorbike. A short time later, Dad bought my five-year-old brother a single-speed RM50 Suzuki, and we became little daredevils on our bikes.

Every chance we had, my brother and I rolled our motorcycles out of the garage and did daredevil feats. We dragged out a few tires and plywood from behind our house, stacking them at one end of the row of friends. With everybody whooping and hollering, I revved up my motorcycle, peeled out with smoke everywhere, and jumped the high ramp with one hand off the handlebars.

To make it suspenseful, I slowly drove around and asked the crowd of cheering and screaming kids circling us who wanted to volunteer as part of the jump show. I chose up to seven kids and had them lie down in the street next to each other. My brother made the crowd roar by telling them it was doubtful if I could do it. I told everyone I hoped I could do it, right before I took off down the street towards the ramp, and sometimes landed within inches of the last kid's head.

When I rode my motorcycle, the sheer adrenaline drove me into a state of maniacal bliss. Feelings of anxiety, restlessness, and fear turned to excitement. Mom was scared to death when we rode our dirt bikes, but bit her tongue.

And since parents thought it silly to pad every square inch of a child's life like nowadays, there was freedom for us to get skinned up, learn from our mistakes, and learn how to do it right. Granted, I am a very careful parent, but back then, it was a whole different world. And for the record, Mom never knew we were jumping friends. I often rode around the neighborhood on my motorcycle, feeling cool with my full pads, helmet, and motocross boots, wondering what the next death-defying stunt could be.

Eventually, Dad moved us again, this time into a double-wide trailer within an hour's drive to the Oregon desert full of cacti, dunes, and desert animals. I thought our trailer was awesome, complete with white siding, brown trim, and an extended kitchen bay window. Having a mobile home was trendy and considered cool in the 1970s. I will never forget the two-inch green and shaggy carpet throughout our doublewide palace.

I liked living in the desert because in the winter and summer, we had direct access to awesome motorbike riding areas. There was lots of space to ride in the desert dunes, and I became very good at climbing hills, jumping over levees, and maneuvering through rocks. My brother became good at pushing the limits of his motorcycle, swooping through the dunes, racing me to imaginary finish lines.

Dad had a Suzuki PE250 and bought a Honda 125 for Mom. My whole family rode together, and it was some of the best times of my young life. My favorite riding experiences I had were at the desert dunes with my family and uncle, except when I almost killed my brother.

My brother and I had been racing up and down a berm and levee all day, and knew of this area to try our feats of fearlessness. It was an awesome place to practice jumping, and we thought it could be fun if both of us came down opposite sides at the same time. We agreed to yell out when one or the other went first, once we arrived at our starting points, hoping that this would ward off any crazy situations. I waited to hear my brother shout, but heard nothing, so I took off.

Gaining speed, I headed right for the edge of the berm and started to descend. My brother also began going down the levee. Because we were going so fast, we froze, and neither of us moved out of the way, our hearts going a hundred miles an hour as we stared in horror.

Meeting at the bottom, our bikes met head-on. When we collided, they lifted in the back, our heads nearly smashed together. We hit so violently that the impact snapped off my brother's brake lever, bent his shocks, front wheel, frame, and broke two of his knuckles. My front forks were dented a little, and the clutch lever was bent.

Physically, I came out okay, other than scrapes and bruises. I was freaking out because I thought my brother was seriously injured. Then he started acting erratically, taking off his helmet and throwing it on the ground. Shoving his motorcycle to one side against the compacted sand floor with a loud "thud," he started quickly looking around at the ground.

I just stared at him, not saying a word. My brother was silent, face squished into an extremely mad pose, acting as if he was halfway delirious. "What are you doing?" I asked, concerned he was out of it and injured. "I am looking for a stick to beat the hell out of you!" he yelled out.

I started laughing so hard I was crying. He had every right to be angry, but that little man was so funny, walking around with his arms out, stomping and huffing between breaths. He was so short that all you could see was a helmet, motocross pads, and boots. I did my best to talk him down from being so mad at me, but he would have nothing of it, grimacing and shouting out loud, "Where is that stick? Where are you, Stick?"

After a few minutes of letting him calm down, we looked over our bikes at the bent and broken parts. Cranking up our bikes, we climbed up the same side this time and took off on the trail again. Slowly, we made our way back to base camp.

Dad and my uncle saw the whole thing, watching as we hobbled and limped our bikes back to the van. Needless to say, Dad saw how sorry we were, hurting and barely making it back. In his way of thinking, having to push our bikes back to the trailer in pain was punishment enough. After all, he was raising tough little men, learning from our mistakes and doing better next time. In our young minds, we were only interested in fun and excitement, unaware of the protection we had that day from God.

Defying the Lies: A Memoir

Chapter 4:

HOPE

Oregon was just another stop along the way to developing and reinforcing my social disorders, but it had its pluses. After school, I usually went outside to play with my skateboard, or anything I could find, due to being grounded often for my motorcycle. I was bad at sneaking out and riding it, and it sucked being limited on things to do.

I had no video games or the other thousands of electronic distractions kids have today. Watching the same five channels on the huge floor television became old fast. Since remote controls did not usually come with televisions, my brother and I had to get up for our parents and change the channel.

In the summer, I found all kinds of rocks under the sand, dirt, and loose gravel next to our trailer, imagining no one had ever found these earth-shattering discoveries. Quartz, fool's gold, and others made my international expeditions worthwhile, running inside to describe and explain the newest additions to my rock collection. Mom, otherwise known as my exclusive scientific community, was always happy to see the latest findings.

There were a lot of kids in the trailer park, but as much as I tried, engaging with other children did not come naturally. It was easier to be alone, letting my mind shift into neutral. I could never figure out what they wanted from me or how to act around them. I guess I was just a young guy who analyzed everything, especially potential connections. Being a little short-tempered and shorter on patience, I usually closed myself off from friends unless I was in control, like ramp jumping.

Often, I escaped into my world. My favorite place to zone out and try to quiet my hectic and racing mind, other than my room, was my homemade monkey bars. They were the tall metal chain link fence surrounding the back of our yard, where no one bugged me.

Climbing to the top of the fence, I draped my legs over the top horizontal pole, falling backwards with my back against the metal links. Looking at my upside-down world, I hung on until blood rushed into my head, feeling the heartbeat pulsing in my ears until it made me let go with my legs. Then I flipped upside down and landed on my hands and knees.

Like many days before, I was zoning out upside down on my imaginary monkey bars. I started to fall asleep and might have fallen straight down on my head if not for this weird kid from next door scuffling fast across his yard. He kicked some rocks across the yard that hit the fence right below my head, scaring the crap out of me, almost making me fall off the fence anyway.

"Hey, look what I got!" he yelled out. I flipped down off the fence, brushed my jeans off, and made my maddest looking face right at him. He always had this crazy look in his eyes, but this time there was this oddly funny grin, too. "What does that creep want?" I mumbled.

He pulled out this small, round metal can with green stickers from his pocket and held it up close to my face. Opening the lid, he said, "Want some?" Inside the round can was this black, smelly stuff that looked like the dirt where I found my fishing worms. "What's that?" I asked with puzzled curiosity.

"It's chew. I snagged it from my dad when he wasn't looking. You want some?" he asked again. But instead of acting like I was wimping out, I just said, "Naw, not right now."

The weirdo kid with long, frazzled hair that defied gravity tilted his head, looked at me with wild, blue-squinted eyes for a few seconds, then ran off laughing, calling me names. I guess he knew I did not want it. Feeling completely rejected, I ran inside looking for Mom.

I had no idea how to deal with what happened, but I knew I needed Mom to help me feel better. She always knew what to do. After getting a drink of water, I walked into her room, and she was bowing her head.

I slowly walked up to Mom and asked what she was doing. She said in her soft, loving voice that she was praying to God about some stuff. Then she stopped, looked at me for a few seconds, and asked what was wrong. Now almost in tears, Mom saw I was rattled about something. She was always aware of our needs and had just the right amount of motherly love and grace.

I told her that the skinny, crazy kid from next door was making fun of me because I did not want any tobacco. Mom hugged and kissed me, saying that it was going to be all right. I did not have to give in to what others did, especially if it was bad. She always had a way of explaining things to me, making me feel so much better.

I asked Mom what praying does for her and what it means to pray to God. She explained that God lived in Heaven and we could pray to Him whenever we had something going on in our lives, helping us through it. Also, when we have Jesus, God's Son, in our lives and, most importantly, in our hearts, He gives us the power to ask and receive when we believe.

I asked how I could have Jesus in my life. She said that in the Bible John 3:16 says, "For God so loved the World that he gave His only begotten Son, that whosoever believes in Him shall not die but have everlasting Life." Mom said Jesus was God's Son who came to this earth to save man from sin.

It was simple! I just needed to ask Jesus into my heart, and He would clean me up, give me a new hope, and I would spend eternity in Heaven. Right then and there, I decided I wanted Jesus to be in my heart, so we prayed together as I repeated what she said:

"Jesus, I am a sinner. I thank you for dying on the Cross to take away my sins. Please forgive me for sinning. I thank you for cleansing me from all unrighteousness and giving me a new heart to serve you, and for walking with me through my life. Thank you for giving me a brand new start. In Jesus' Name, Amen."

I smiled, hugged mom, and told her I felt new and clean. The very next day, we went to the skating rink, and I was so happy that I shared my experience, but people did not want to hear what I wanted to say. Then I remembered what mom told me, saying if I was saved, struggles and rejections would happen, but God is always by my side.

Chapter 5:

FIRST GRADE LLAMA

It is funny what you remember. It can be good, bad, and horrible, or all at the same time. Speaking of horrible, when I started first grade, I met Mrs. Veers. Mrs. Veers had to have been all of eighty if even a day. She was the one instructor every kid dreaded to get, and parents heard she was hard to get along with. Unfortunately, it was inevitable that every student had to pass through her class to get to the next grade level because it was such a small school district. She taught math, science, English, Social Studies, and Basic Writing, and the last class terrified me.

Mrs. Veers always looked like she was in pain while walking, having to stop constantly to lean on desks after only a few feet. With her thick coke-bottle glasses, I wondered how she even saw us talking or acting out. She was overweight and had big slobbering lips that pushed

Defying the Lies: A Memoir

out words in a forced movement like a cow trying to speak. This weird, brown always covered her lips, lining the top and bottom of them. Perhaps it was tobacco stains from chewing tobacco, but we never did solve the mystery of the brown lips.

As she taught, Mrs. Veers spoke in broken and slurred English as she weaved in and out of our desks. No one knew where she would end up, so we followed her every move. Kids all over the room became signal senders and lookouts for one another, being careful not to let her catch us looking while she meandered. Every time she opened her lips to speak, thick, semi-transparent milky fluid started oozing out of the edges of her mouth. We cringed as she told us to stop messing around, yelling, and mumbling wet words of slobber that never made any real sense.

The first-grade Llama's "spit ammo" was extremely accurate, too. She was always loaded up in her wrinkled, puffy cheeks for whichever student was misbehaving or had the wrong answer. Mrs. Veers was constantly ready to spray out in steady automatic streams from between those huge lips, spitting at any and every innocent bystander. It was every boy and girl for themselves, and no one was safe.

On a rainy Wednesday school morning, it was time to learn this new type of writing called cursive. I had seen the same scribbling at home on one of dad's yellow work pads, and ever since, I wanted to learn it. Stretching across the entire top of the long black chalkboard were white and yellow scribblings of subjects taught throughout the day. Right below it was a long white rectangular piece of paper with every letter of the alphabet in large and small curly-looking symbols written on it.

I looked at Mrs. Veers with sheer terror. I did not move a muscle or make a single sound when she asked the class if anyone had seen this sort of writing before. I had heard the classroom horror stories on the playground of kids not being able to learn cursive because it was very scary, so I did not say a word.

Rumor had it that a few students were even relocated to another school and never heard from again, due to emotional scarring. Slowly, her dark, beady eyes started scanning back and forth across the room of students as she started to sway, getting ready to ask them her devious questions. Sweat started pouring off my forehead as panic overtook my body.

Mrs. Veers started walking from her desk, head swiveling ever so slightly. Her entire body creaked and cracked more than the old wooden floor beneath her while snaking her way between our desks. She was definitely on a mission of search and destroy, wandering about the room to see who might be the next victim of harassment and ridicule.

Then out of nowhere, she spun around and shouted, "Ha! I see you there!" shooting out her bony index finger right at this little blonde girl cowering behind a boy's large curly-covered head. Mrs. Veers asked her to point out the small cursive letter "h." The little girl luckily said the right answer, narrowly escaping utter wrath. Unfortunately, I sat right behind her.

I just stayed frozen solid in my desk as Mrs. Veers started moving again, sweat now pouring down my back, my eyes transfixed on the chalkboard in front of me. I kept saying under my breath, "Not me, not me, not me." Suddenly out of nowhere, she was right beside me, bent down in an awkward slant with her neck cocked and dark eyes staring into my soul. In a low scratchy voice, she said, "Which one is the cursive version of the small letter C, Eric?"

My mouth felt so dry it felt like cotton, and I could not open my mouth to utter a single sound. I looked up at the chart, swallowed hard, and answered, "The second big letter." I turned and nervously squinted at her with my teeth clenched, waiting to see what would happen next. Mrs. Veers leaned in very close to me with a devilish grin, her lips loaded up with milky spit oozing from the corners of her mouth, and yelled into my ear, "NO, NO!" with screeching repetition.

Without warning, a continuously thick viscous spray shot from her mouth. Before I could say "duck and cover!" it coated my face and several students' bodies on my left and right. Still mumbling and shaking her head, she scuffled away to the blackboard while we wiped off the mucus from our faces, counting the casualties.

I started stuttering very badly after this incident. Working very hard with mom and going to speech therapy, it took a few years to overcome it. Mom was very patient and loving, praying and helping me along the way in the same manner as when she helped me read. I could not have overcome this speech disability without her patience, love, and mercy, a definite, selfless gift from a woman who always put her children first.

Chapter 6:

SNAKES

I know I attended at least two different middle schools, a Christian school and a public one, and another one, maybe. I can not recall teachers, friends, or classrooms other than loving to go down a large metal slide in the middle of wintertime. I also distinctly recall being bullied by the private school's well-known preacher's kid, then going home and escaping into my room, shutting myself off from the world. This was my safe place, and I could control what happened there. As long as nothing changed within my bubble, I did not get that upset.

I often disappeared into my world of fantasy, making stories up about practically anything. It was a type of self-medication. It kind of worked until reality stepped in, suffering with severe rejection, usually brought on by my skewed perception.

Whenever we moved, I tried to keep my immediate world, namely my room, perfectly straight and organized. In third grade, I developed the dysfunction of crying anytime I was disappointed or let down and would scream out, becoming erratic. I also stayed away from mom and dad when I was told of any changes.

If I asked to sleep over at someone's house, I felt rejected when their parents said no, thinking they hated me. I remember distinctly this kid acting funny because I started to whine when his mom said, "No." This produced a disdainful hate for people, generalized to anyone who did not do what I wanted or did not agree with my decisions. People got on my nerves, and I usually decided to stay away from them.

I became obsessive-compulsive and hated to see anything in my room that was dirty. It further messed with how I viewed relationships with the opposite sex. I was aware of girls at an early age and liked them very much. Because they acted differently than I thought they should, I ignored any chance to become their friends.

I could not be bothered with their silliness and flighty attitudes. It was a skewed way of perceiving potential friends, resulting in being alone often and separated from others. But again, I had to have things perfectly in order, even the way people acted.

It affected me at home, too. When dad was angry or when mom and dad were fighting, I would cry and plead with them to stop, trying to make everything perfectly calm. I took on false responsibility, telling mom and dad I could do lawn work, wash the dishes, whatever they wanted, if they would just stop arguing.

I honestly cannot tell you how many places we had temporary housing in Louisiana, or a place to store whatever belongings we had left after selling or giving our stuff away, again and again. I do remember there was a yellow house out in the middle of a field that had an old shed where we stored our stuff that mildewed, because it was nasty and leaked water. Dad arranged to finish running the electrical wiring to set up the means for the electricity, getting the lights and utilities turned on in exchange for rent, just like many other times before. But that sort of deal fell through like many others. Dad always believed people would keep their word and never believed in contracts.

Then, Dad found this old farmhouse in Louisiana with an abandoned dairy shed down a short dirt trail on the back part of the land. My brother and I were told to stay away from the old milking building, but of course, we played in it anyway. Inside, it had all of the original milk pumps, ramps, and equipment.

Although it flooded out there, I snuck out and played in the old dairy as many times during the week as I could; after lunch, dinner, or when I had to cut the grass. Whenever it rained, the fields all around the farm flooded, completely saturating everything and welcoming slithery, poisonous snakes called water moccasins. Every time after it rained, snakes appeared everywhere.

It became a game when I cut grass to see how many I could slice up into pieces before stray dogs came to the farm, trying to catch the slithery creatures.

Sometimes, I took a Triton pitchfork used to catch bullfrogs to stab them before the dogs attacked. Let me tell you, God protected me more than once from getting bitten. One day, I was snake hunting at the edge of our property and climbed through a hole in the barbed-wire fence that ran along the left side of the farmhouse. Yeah, I was told not to do this, but well, you know.

As a parent, you have an inherent feeling when your child is disobeying. I was walking around in the tall weeds when Dad yelled out to me, "I'd better not find you crawling through the barbed wire!" I heard him and quickly started crawling back through the fence when the skin of my leg under my jeans caught on a piece of the razor wire, slicing my leg wide open, leaving a pretty good-sized gash.

I screamed out to dad, who was working in the yard, and he came running around the side of the house, seeing me hung up by this wire. He took his pliers, cut them from around my jeans and leg, and helped me stand up away from the fence. There was little bleeding, which was surprising. It was a clean, wide hole sliced open that I thought should have been much worse. There was only a little pain, as if you pricked your finger, and it was not as bad as it looked.

When we went to the hospital, a surgeon looked at my leg and brought me immediately back to a room to get stitched up. The doctor told me to put my hands under my legs and relax. When I felt the first stick of the needle right into the middle of the wound, I screamed and passed out.

I woke up just as the doctor was finishing up the last few stitches. He just glanced over at me and said calmly, "Oh, he's awake now." Dad looked at me, smiled, then turned to watch the doctor do his thing. Both of them acted like it was just another normal day. Yeah, it was the 1970s.

It was funny how Dad viewed discipline. Although neglecting my needs for stability as a child, he knew how to handle these situations. If we injured ourselves while not following directions, like when my brother and I crashed our motorcycles, it was a lesson learned. He saw that the best way to teach us was to feel the consequences of our actions. It worked because I never, ever went through that barbed-wire fence again.

Defying the Lies: A Memoir

Chapter 7:

BLACK DEATH

We moved from the hot and humid Louisiana countryside to Oregon, where a ton of snow and ice fell every winter. Over seven feet high, snow drifts piled up on each side of the roads when the truck scrapers came through the neighborhoods. One Saturday afternoon, severe snowstorms had been blowing throughout the morning, so going outside was not an option.

I was playing with Hot Wheels when Dad popped his head into my room, asking if I wanted to go dump trash with him. I immediately said "Yes!" because I loved riding in his big white work truck. It had sliding doors that I opened up as we drove along the highway, and this made me feel free and daring. Another bonus was that we were not going to do regular electrical work like digging ditches in frozen ground, setting up huge spools of wire, or drilling endless rows of holes in three-story wooden house frames.

    Mom told us to be careful because there was a snow and ice storm earlier that morning, and the ice beneath the snow was forming quickly into a very hazardous situation. She kissed me on my cheek, making sure my big coat was buttoned up snugly over my overalls. We loaded up the van and took off.

    Sitting in the passenger seat made me feel powerful and important, watching the world fly by the open doors, sticking out my arm to feel the freezing air push against my gloved hand. When people looked at us at stop lights, I nodded at them like I was the one in charge, looking around the cab and puffing out my skinny chest. This was one of the times Dad was fun to be around, when he saw his kiddos having fun. Deep down, I knew he loved me, trying to make up for the crappy times of moving us everywhere and working us all of the time, but doing things like this.

    We stopped and picked up my uncle and said a prayer for God to protect us. Heading to the country dump site, I moved and sat on the dashboard, facing the back of the van. My uncle situated himself in the passenger seat. Because the roads were made of asphalt, the ice froze on the surface, becoming invisible. Everywhere you drove was very hazardous because when road crews tried to scrape the snow away, a thin layer froze and melted onto the ice already present.

    These frozen, solid asphalt roads, called black ice, take the lives of people every year. It was very unfortunate for some, not surviving accidents on the evasive unseen "black death." I turned around to the front of the van, nervously looking out of the big, square front two windshields as we approached the dump. Earlier, dad was playing around and fishtailed, so my stomach was in knots as I tried to see the black ice in front of us. Uneasiness turned into terror when, driving around the last curve, a gigantic truck, hauling a fifteen-ton garbage bin, moved into our lane. Dad yelled out, "God help me!" as he gripped the steering wheel, turning it to the right so the truck could hit on his side. As the truck came closer with all fourteen of its wheels now in our lane, Dad managed to get the left front of the van turned into the oncoming truck in only a matter of a few seconds.

I quickly turned around and closed my eyes, waiting for the crash. My uncle braced himself in the little fold-down passenger seat. The feeling of both trucks coming together was indescribable, combined with piercing sounds of smashing metal, aluminum, glass, and steel. My body went limp, then complete silence.

I opened my eyes slowly in shock, looking at my uncle, who had already unhooked himself from the seat and went over to where Dad was crushed. The eighteen-ton garbage truck collided with Dad's side, taking all of the impact. Our van's engine was shoved up underneath the aluminum dash, pinning dad's legs up to his hips inside of a crumpled, smoking pile of metal. Police later stated the other driver's cab had smashed into ours so deeply that the initial contact distance between both drivers' heads was estimated to have been less than a foot.

Seeing the dashboard pinning dad's legs, my uncle started praying, supernaturally gaining enough strength to push the inch-thick, solid aluminum piece up and away from him. As soon as this happened, Dad's ankles broke free from the painful position. Then my Uncle started praying as I turned away when I heard the loud snap from the pressure release of his bones. I looked out the front of the van, where both windshields were somehow missing.

Dad was pinned tight in his seat while his legs, knees, and ankles were bloody, full of glass, jeans material, shards of metal, and broken bone. There were long, sharp poles called grounding rods used to penetrate hard ground and rock previously stored in the back of the truck. They punched through the cab divider wall and into the back of Dad's seat. The rods barely missed his body, ending up on each side of Dad's back, cutting the lower left and right corners of his shirt.

I was sitting in the same spot where I was before the wreck, but my right boot was jammed between the destroyed floor shifter and the bottom of the aluminum engine cover. I managed to pull my boot and foot free from it as a policeman showed up in our van doorway. He helped me climb down and out of the truck and very carefully over to the cop car.

Emergency crews arrived shortly after the police, getting Dad pulled from the truck and into the ambulance. I was scared, crying, and confused because I did not want Dad to die and had no idea what was happening. On the way to the police car parked several feet up the icy hill from the wreckage, the policeman asked me if I had a jacket to keep warm. Looking around, I told him that I lost it.

We were all transported by ambulance to the hospital and checked out. Dad was messed up, needing several months of rehabilitation. The doctor looked at my uncle, and he was determined to be fine.

I had a dark purple bruise on my hip, but other than

being shaken up, doctors found nothing else wrong. I had an X-ray of my hip bone and ligaments during a doctor follow-up a few months later and was ultimately cleared of any health issues. I have never, ever had anything wrong with my hip other than a little soreness for the first year or so after the wreck. Having had no therapy, surgeries, or any corrective action performed, I squatted over four hundred pounds as a bodybuilder, knowing God healed me.

My uncle told me that I flipped completely backwards towards the front windows upon impact. With arms flailing outwards, my elbows hit and shatter both windshields as my jacket came off, ending up under the rear wheels of the other truck twenty-five feet away. I did not move with the inertia of our van but flipped in midair and miraculously ended up sitting exactly the way I was before we hit the truck. Somehow, God kept me inside the cab. According to accident examiners and cops, at the scene that day, I should have been killed by being thrown from the van and rolled over by the garbage truck.

Chapter 8:

FOOTBALL FREAK

After we picked up and transitioned to Louisiana from Oregon, again, I was sent to one of two high schools for my first two years. We had nine hundred and thirty-nine freshmen students in my first school. It was a huge student body with my class filling half of the gym. The sophomores, juniors, and seniors sat on the other side. If you think someone could get confused and lost in that giant sea of people, you are right.

Built in the 1920s, the old high school with auxiliary buildings was a huge circle with classes all around the outer rim and the gym in the middle. If a student became lost, all they had to do was walk around the school to find his or her class. But that was not the case for me.

Attention Deficit Hyperactivity Disorder (ADHD) caused my mind to never stop going a hundred miles an hour with a thousand different thoughts, so it was hard to find my way. I was always turned around in the halls, and once I made it to class, concentrating on anything being taught was hopeless. My struggle was very tough when I tried to focus and suffered with ADHD, inducing panic and fear, starting from junior high.

I told Mom I was having a really hard time learning anything or focusing. I always heard the teachers talking, kids whispering from across the room, and noises outside the windows all at the same time. I continuously looked around to see what was causing the noises, never caught what was being taught, and no matter how hard I tried, I forgot what I was reading or what the teacher was talking about. As a result, I disappeared into a daydreaming world, thinking about anything and everything else except seventh-grade schoolwork.

Mom brought me to the doctor to see if there was something that could be done. We talked to him for a while about what I was experiencing in school and how concentration was impossible on any schoolwork. Being a doctor who was a strong advocate of prescription medication, he suggested I try some new drugs being experimented with on other children also having trouble focusing.

Mom eventually agreed for me to try it, and I was given medication to start taking that evening. And man, it screwed me up. After two weeks, the medication started working too well, making me slow way down. I felt like I was walking in a deep, slow fog, but still not understanding or comprehending anything.

Sitting at my desk at school with a dead stare and eyes glazed over, I saw the teachers' mouths move, but I did not grasp anything. To me, it was low, slow mumbling in my ears. All the distracting background sounds, noises, and voices faded into silence, and that was good, but when trying to listen to my parents or others, I might as well have been underwater. I also felt as if the world around me was creeping along, slowing way down.

I talked slower, and sometimes I had to think hard about what I was going to do or say next. Remembering names and what I was going to say became a little easier, but it took a long time to come out of my mouth. After a month of this craziness, I told my mom what was happening, so we went back to the doctor to let him know what was going on with my health.

According to the doctor, what I experienced was normal, caused by this now explained legal form of speed that calmed and focused hyper children. This pharmaceutical also slowed down a person's brain that processed too quickly and could not concentrate on one task at a time. The medicine I was taking screwed me up, perhaps from not having the right levels in my blood or the right medication altogether.

In either case, I hated it, and Mom was very concerned that it made me worse in other areas. We all agreed to take me off of it, and I was more than glad to do it. I know Mom meant well, realizing I could have worse problems entering high school in a few years.

What I soon learned about high school was that it took no prisoners, chewing up and spitting out its hapless freshmen victims. Bullying was the order of the day, and if anyone was a prime target, I was. I seemed to attract it like a magnet.

I had also developed a victim mentality, meaning I would cower and shuffle down the hallways, thinking I was worthless, head hung low, acting like no one liked me. Students seemed really good at picking up on my insecure behavior, calling me every name imaginable. It was hell.

I had to do something to fit in while making my way through the daily barrages of getting hammered. Yes, it was a pretty normal thing for new students to pick on you, but it was especially rough for me because I held onto everything bad said to me. I adopted all of the negativity as my persona and believed it more than myself.

My brother was pretty athletic from a young age, becoming an all-state gymnast as a preteen, and he always had friends. I figured if being athletic made him get friends, then I would do it, too. So, as a twelve-year-old, I started doing push-ups, running, sit-ups, and using the weight set dad bought. When I turned thirteen, I was able to lift weights at a gym near our house. Slowly but surely, I started filling out my skinny frame and developed some semblance of identity and confidence.

It was nearing the fall season of my freshman year, and football games were coming. One of my teachers taught Biology and was the defensive football coach. On a Friday before dismissing us, he said football tryouts would be held the following week. Anyone who wanted to see if they had what it took to be a part of the team could come out and go through the paces.

The following Monday, I went to tryouts, along with lots of other students. Coaches had their pick of dozens of freshmen chosen to grow and learn with the team for the next four years, some undoubtedly set to become their future senior starters. I tried my hardest to hit, run, and catch.

As bad as I was, I ended up making the team. We had a huge football program with second, third, and fourth string, eighty-five students in all. Getting chosen was pretty much a given.

Every football practice, the crap was kicked out of me, but I did not care. Still working out and growing taller, I was also bigger and stronger. I volunteered every practice to hold a tall, round pad that players hit while going through play drills, called a dummy.

Regardless of how hard I was hit or how many times I was pounded to the ground, quitting was not for me, no matter what. Every day after school, I put on my football pads and would go outside to get beaten up at practice. It was a pretty good feeling despite bruises and cuts, knowing I was part of something bigger than myself.

As much as I wanted to be a part of the team, I was not good at remembering the plays or learning practice moves. Up until this point, I had sheltered myself socially, staying away from others. I did not understand that to be a part of the team meant sharing and engaging with other players outside of practice and games. I never talked to any of the football players during school time, and they perceived me as being stuck up or not liking them. Being unsociable discounted my desire to be accepted in football, and I became continuously reclusive, once again.

I was a ridiculously lousy football player and a terrible friend to others on the team because of my dismissive, accusatory attitude towards anyone who dared talk to me, or said I was something I was not. It was my defense mechanism to avoid them before getting hurt. Anyway, I constantly forgot everything I learned in the field, mixing up strategy and play names in my head because of my social instability and ADHD. I screwed up in practice, especially when the coach asked me where to go during a play. I felt intimidated by him and by the players making fun of me.

On top of everything else, I began developing intermittent panic attacks. Down every hall and in every classroom, I sweated constantly, my heartbeat jumping out of my chest, breathing heavily while seeing everyone as enemies. I was living in emotional turmoil, but my parents never knew what I was experiencing. Just like elementary school, I had no idea how to tell them. Mom knew when I was bothered or upset, but when she asked me what was wrong, I simply said "nothing," quietly disappearing into my room.

Walking outside in large, open spaces in front of people in the school courtyard was the worst for me. I avoided them all, from groups of people talking to each other, football players discussing upcoming football games, or anyone else that I might have known from classes who wanted me to hang out. Students around the school talking and carrying on were a constant blur of confusion and useless chatter in my mind.

I just walked by everyone with my eyes closed and head down. I kept to myself, shutting off the outside world as much as possible. It was a constant refusal of will, having a torturous emotional fight within me.

When I dressed out in the locker rooms for football practice, I hated it. Kids commented on my thick red hair, asking me when I was going to get a haircut, and bullied me with names because I was socially awkward. Nothing was off-limits. In hindsight, they were just being kids, but when you expect nothing but negative comments about who you are, then that is what you hear. I did not know how to let things roll off my back or give it back to them, so I took things extremely personally, avoided everyone, absorbed the negativity, and made it part of my identity.

My grades really suffered too, making a D and sometimes an F in classes, even with tutors. I never remembered math concepts, English passages, history lessons, and others. Every fundamental rule of curriculum and instruction seemed trivial to me, and standardized tests were a mystery.

When I barely made it to my sophomore year of high school, my anger, emotional instability, and psychological issues became worse. No matter how hard I tried not to freak out, I lost it and did stupid stuff like smashing mom's furniture or punching a hole in the wall. I always felt like a cannon about to go off, and sometimes it did.

As I started working out harder and feeling stronger, I scared Dad more than once by screaming and walking towards him. Dad just walked away, not knowing what to do when I eventually exploded. I would blank out when I became enraged, and at school, people stared at me and walked away. Gradually, my active anger became passive-aggressive, and I was very good at quick-witted, sarcastic remarks without blowing up at people or damaging things.

Instead of my anger getting under control, it became subversive, showing itself through passive comments during class towards teachers. I sat in the back and spouted out something stupid or made dumb noises to make myself look and feel better in front of others. Truth is, all this crap going on only fueled the hate for myself.

One hot, sunny day during my sophomore year, the football team was going over punt-return exercises, and I was on the offensive team. I became so pissed off during one of the drills that I called everyone communists. Well, when you call a bunch of flag-loving, Cajun boys that name, it never goes over very well. At the punt, I started running up the field to defend against the opposing practice team when four teammates came close together, heading straight for me.

I kept running, crouched down and eyes closed, until feeling the impact of being hit by the largest guys. They slammed into me, picked me up, knocked me off my feet backwards several feet, and I hit the ground with a heavy "thud!". When I woke up to reality, my helmet face mask was crushed, my chin scraped, and my jaw swollen from several hard-rubber spiked cleats stomping on my face. A doctor visit the next day revealed I had sustained a slight concussion. I never reported the, who did it, and viewed this entire experience as a learning moment. from the Lord.

Chapter 9:

ACTING THE PART

In the summer before my junior year, we moved back across the United States from Louisiana to Tennessee. At least we did not have to go back and forth from Oregon to Louisiana again. The first place we lived was an old two-story Confederate house with lots of rooms, closets, and fireplaces. I liked that old house, and the yard was huge. The wood exterior was covered with faded blue vinyl siding, and it was in a rich part of the neighborhood.

Our neighbors were pretty cool, but then I wrecked their four-wheeler, and we moved a few months later. I always thought I was the reason for the move, and if Dad ever paid for the bike. The house was down the street from some famous country music stars, whose dad did a few independent electrical jobs for them and even built a music studio for one of the leading lyricists in Nashville at the time. I even went to school with a few of the stars' kids, but we never made a big deal about it, since we saw them often around town.

Then came some nice condominiums, but we did not have much stuff besides dishes, the family beds, and an old stereo where my brother loved to play his Phil Collins cassette tape. When dad's deal was done with the owners of the condos, we moved next door to these nasty, run-down apartments that had mold and mildew. At least I had monkey bars behind the crappy apartments to do pull-ups. It was not much, a small kids' play set, but it kept me feeling better. Next, we moved into a small white house with an open car garage in a neighborhood, much like the one we lived in one of the times in Oregon.

At the time we moved to this house, I had been using Dad's old weights and going to the gym. I was six feet, one hundred and eighty pounds of muscle at this point, able to bench press two hundred and twenty-five pounds for twenty reps. God blessed me with strength, and I was stronger than I looked.

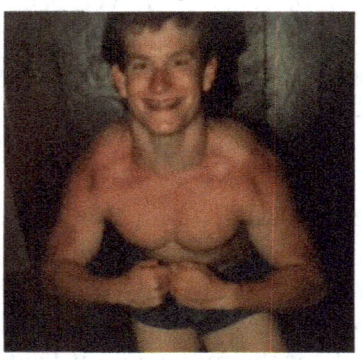

Hanging around with others who worked out actually became friends, something I had not had in any real sense. It was great to have similar things in common. It also gave me a sense of importance and immediate reward with the gains I saw from my body. I loved the feeling of accomplishment that pushing heavy weights gave me and the way it helped to develop a sense of importance in the eyes of others.

Bodybuilding also helped me to develop a sense of

positive self-awareness that I had not experienced before. The summer between my sophomore and junior year, I began to accept myself for me, although still battling a horrendous self-image. People were attracted to me and wanted to talk, but because I was terribly shy and still judgmental, I sometimes avoided it. Women liked what they saw, but my awkwardness did not reflect my outward appearance.

Because I was a pretty big guy, Dad suggested we visit a college to see about me being a football walk-on or a potential scouting prospect. I was looked at by a few coaches and players, although I knew I would not play football for them. It was more about wanting to gain acceptance and feeling important to others, rather than the love of the game.

One afternoon on the high school football field, we were running through offensive and defensive drills. I was lined up across from one of the defensive players, about the same size as me. Over and over, we did the same drills, hits, and plays. Then something snapped inside my head. I became pissed off, but instead of reacting by trying to hit the opposing player harder, I started crying uncontrollably.

I became completely emotionally unhinged, crying like a big freaking baby. It was ridiculous. The more I tried to stop him, the more I balled, and the harder the guy hit me. I felt powerless and quit hitting back, letting him push me farther and farther back from the line of scrimmage.

I could have easily defeated him, but inside, I felt like I was that freshman player who could not stand up, being knocked down like a practice dummy. Something in my head broke, shut down, and turned off. All at once, I stopped caring about anything and everything concerning football. I walked up to the coach and told him I did not want to be on the team anymore. He asked me if I was sure and could still practice with them if I wanted to give it another try.

I looked at the coach sobbing, lowering and shaking my head, and said I was sure. He nodded, turned around, and, walking away, told me to put my gear in the field house. I walked off the field knowing that playing football would never happen again. Maybe it was the concussion injury in my sophomore year rearing its head. Maybe it was my emotional immaturity, but probably both caused all of it.

With football finished, I often became very bored and restless, fidgeting and feeling anxiety rise up inside me if I did not stay busy. Whenever mom saw me shuffling around my room or mindlessly walking around the house, she suggested that I go outside to work out. This always helped me feel better, so the old weight set I used when I first began my weightlifting journey was a welcome relief.

My old red Honda motorcycle, now broken down just feet from my workout place, sat on the back patio. I looked at it between sets, remembering the fun times in Oregon, amid life's struggles and constant changes. Doing exercises in the outdoors was a brief emotional reprieve, remembering the awesome times we had riding motorcycles, and reflecting on these memories helped me to temporarily reset emotionally during my workouts.

Throughout the rest of my high school career, my anxiety, ADHD, emotional insecurities, and bad self-interpretations flared up now and then, creating opportunities to stay hidden away from dating. I did not ask any girls out, never became long-term friends with people, and hid in the gym. I refused to face the fact that I was my own worst enemy, and self-sheltered every chance that came along.

During my freshman, sophomore, and junior years, I barely managed to stay afloat in my grades. My senior year, however, I had two classes that I was failing miserably: Elizabethan Literature and Geometry. They were huge graduation roadblocks and were going to cost me my graduation.

Because I saw no way to finish school on time, my only choices were to repeat my senior year or drop out of school and earn a Graduation Equivalent Diploma (GED). Neither option was one I wanted to think about or even consider. I felt hopeless in my warped mind, thinking of how much worse I would be treated repeating my senior year!

I had had enough of freaking high school and needed to move on to see what else life offered. This phase had to go, and I was hopelessly pissed off. For whatever reason, something deep in my soul said, "No More!"

One day at the gym, I was thinking and worrying about graduation. Suddenly, it clicked in my brain to somehow use the lessons of not quitting at the gym as a scrawny kid, and seeing my muscle-building results years later. I chose to focus on passing school regardless of how bad things looked in the present. It was either quit trying or never, ever stop until I passed. Deciding on the latter, I made up my mind to overcome, no matter what happened.

As a senior, thankfully, I had a few elective choices. Math classes sucked, and of course, concentrating on Geometry or memorizing was completely out of the question. Because my grades were in the trash, the counselor allowed me to take a remedial math class. I thought it was a humiliating selection because students who were not mentally capable were enrolled at this level, a fundamental mathematics course designed for very low-functioning individuals.

I had nothing against those in these sorts of classes because they needed them. I just thought I was above that entire sort of stuff. I was not.

Swallowing my pride, I took the math class and made top honors in it with a ninety-seven percent. The front office placed my name, grade, and a congratulatory message that read, "Congratulations, Eric Parr, for a Perfect Grade of A in Your Mathematics Class!" high up on the message board next to the main highway. Embarrassed but feeling good, I was done with math. People in the front office congratulated me, hugged me, and gave me high-fives. The counselor and principal were proud of me, and I felt accepted.

The other class I was failing was one that I had not thought through during the class selection process. Why I chose Literature, I will never know. For some reason, I thought I could do this subject, but it was a lot more difficult than it first appeared, having historical references about Elizabethan Literature.

For my final, the teacher allowed us to take her test or prepare a presentation of personal experience. This was a miracle out of nowhere. I chose to do a speech on steroids and bodybuilding,

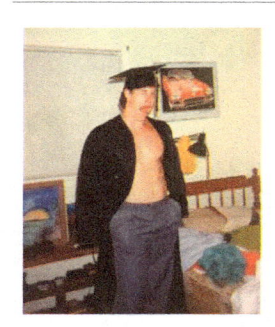

Being a gifted natural weightlifter, I was blessed with strength from both sides of my family. I worked out with some people who were not, and they chose to take steroids, almost dying. This subject was close to my heart, and I was a strong advocate for natural ways to get stronger. I made an "A" on my final and graduated high school by the skin of my teeth.

Chapter 10:

FUN NAVY TORTURE

About a year before I joined the military, I worked in a movie theater and some restaurants, but they were dead-end jobs, and I was not going anywhere. Deciding to get out of town and learn something, I started school at Volunteer State Community College, not far from home. Then I moved away to attend two others, seeking all of my collegiate options.

After trying out a few schools, I realized I was neither ready nor motivated academically for college, no matter where I was trying to attend. Making friends did become easier as I continued to build on my ability to believe in myself, becoming more open to developing friendships as I grew personally and spiritually. College, in a social sense, seemed to come more naturally to me than high school, but not being satisfied with pursuing college at this point, I searched out other opportunities.

I was driving around town one afternoon, getting lost as usual. That old habit of not knowing where I was, even in familiar territory, still haunted me. I turned into this shopping center trying to find the grocery store when I saw a sign that read, "Naval Recruiting Office," in big blue letters on a white sign right when I walked inside.

Something deep inside of me clicked. I can not explain it, but I knew beyond a shadow of a doubt that I was going to join the military. I sped home and told mom and dad I saw a Navy poster at the grocery store and decided, then and there, I wanted to join.

Dad, being an Air Force veteran, looked right at me and, surprisingly, said it was a great idea. He had been a person in the past who often dismissed others' ideas, many times mine, but not about the military. Mom suddnly had a concerned and sad look in her eyes, but did not say anything. I knew mom was upset, but she knew it was time for me to get out and start my life.

In a few days, Dad and I went to New Orleans to the Military Entrance Processing Station (MEPS). This was the central screening unit where every future military person had to go for health checks, tests for jobs, extensive blood workups, and an overall physical health assessment. People also went there to swear into the military according to their chosen branch: Army, Navy, Air Force, Marines, Coast Guard, and all reserve units of the Armed Forces.

The military processing was very lengthy and intense. Nurses and doctors did many physical, psychological, and emotional workups to ensure that I was ready for the training and lifestyle. From weightlifting to calisthenics, I was put through many, many rigorous paces to make sure I could handle the Navy way of life.

I gave countless tubes of blood, and they were submitted to the nurses. I also gave a urine sample to make sure illegal drugs were not in my bloodstream. Potential health risk questionnaires were filled out, and verbal interviews were performed to guarantee I had no previous health issues or detrimental injuries. Throughout the entire process, I walked through countless doors, down hallway after hallway. Eventually, I came to a corridor. It opened up into an area where a nurse behind a tall desk was verifying names, dates, social security numbers, and matching blood types and results to military hopefuls.

When I walked up to the desk, the nurse asked for my name, looked for my chart, opened it, and suddenly looked puzzled. He said something was off with my lab results, and he had to recheck a few things. A short time later, he returned to his station and said everything was fine, and I could proceed through the rest of MEPS. I was more nervous now but relieved, and walked on to the rest of the tests. I never did find out what spooked the nurse.

The last stop in MEPS was to pick out my job, or rate, in the Navy. Based on my test scores and availability of military careers, my choices were to be a submarine navigator, an Aircrew Survival Equipmentman (PR), or a parachute rigger. This was the nickname/acronym given to what the job was, but I would learn it encompassed an infinite amount of gear and expertise. Not wanting to be in an electrified, mechanical metal tube at the bottom of the ocean for six months out of the year, I chose to work on aircrew survival equipment.

With qualifications completed and my rate picked, I went to the swear-in hall where every recruit who qualified to join the military of every branch would raise their right hand and take the oath. I left MEPS as a United States Navy recruit, eager to start my military journey. I was on my way to begin a new adventure.

As soon as I returned home, I told Mom I had just joined the Navy. She started pacing around the living room and suddenly broke down crying. Mom was very upset because I said before leaving the house, I was only going to check it out, but not sign on the dotted line. Mom was right to feel that way, and I was sorry, but I knew this was what I had to do.

I was completely sold on the idea of joining the military, and nothing was going to stop me. Being at home was not an option anymore. I had no direction, no solid personal realization of who I was or where I was going in life.

Mom eventually understood my wanting to head to the high seas, but with hidden reluctance. Her "baby boy" was leaving the house, and things were changing. All things considered, it was past time for my life to evolve, to grow beyond the present into what God wanted me to be.

I was in the Navy Delayed Entry Program (NDEP), going every week to my Navy recruiter's office to learn about rank, military bearing, and talk to other people who were interested in joining up, too. It was a great learning experience and time to get prepared. I knew, according to the recruiter, surprises abounded once I started training, but I did what I could to minimize the initial training impact, or so I thought.

Over the following months, I prepared my mind as best I could for boot camp, watching naval television programs, movies, studying hard in my delayed entry program, and exercising to be in the best shape I could before leaving for training. In January of 1992, I received the call. After nine months of waiting and studying preliminary military information, rank, watch standing rules, and general protocol, I would finally be heading off to the Navy in February. My recruiting petty officer, who was over the delayed entry program, told me over the phone that I would be shipping off to Great Lakes, Illinois, for boot camp.

Being that it was only a month before I would ship off to Navy training, Mom and Dad's church decided to get together and throw me a going-away party. It was bittersweet seeing my parents talking to their friends about who I was, what I was going to do, and how proud they were of me. I had not seen this side of my dad before, and he seemed excited to see me going off and making something of myself. My mom did her best "mom" happiness despite being sad.

It turned out to be a good time with lots of great food and conversation. I hung out with my little brother, whom I had not seen in a while, because he was away at college. At this stage in our lives, we were doing our own thing: I was heading off to the Navy, and my brother was moving away again to finish school. He was the epitome of the early nineties, and we could not have been more opposite. I was a recluse and weightlifter, and he was a pretty boy socialite who knew it and was a charmer to the ladies. But regardless of our differences, we were close and had a great time catching up on what we had been doing over the last few years.

I hung out with mom, sharing memories of growing up, and received some great advice. Mom was never a woman of many words, but when she spoke, it was always insightful and perceptive. Overall, the get-together was a great final send-off to help relax my overly analytical brain and prepare mentally for boot camp.

Soon, February came along, and it was time to start my new life. I packed my duffel bag complete with the list of stuff my Delayed Entry Petty Officer gave to me, loaded up the car, and headed to the New Orleans International Airport. On the way there, it was a relaxing yet anxious trip as I sat in the back seat looking out the window, wondering what would come next. Mom and Dad asked if I knew what I would be doing once I arrived at boot camp. I had no idea, shaking my head in silence, lost in my thoughts of what was to come.

The hour-long journey flew by, and before I knew it, we had arrived at the airport. We parked and all of us went directly to the terminal so I would not be late boarding the plane. Back in those days, the fear of dangerous activities by crazy people was not on anyone's radar, so you could hang out right by the aircraft loading ramp doors. It was a completely different era where families and friends had a better experience with picking up and dropping off at the gate.

We arrived about fifty minutes before my plane took off, and Mom, with her quiet, quick wit and funny jokes that most of the time only she understood, helped to make me feel at ease. I appreciated what she was doing and tried to laugh through my anxiousness. Dad was proud and smiling, looking around the airport and keeping track of when it was time for me to board.

After many years of struggles, miraculous events, confusion, and turmoil, overcoming impossible situations, this chapter of my life was closing, and another was opening up. I could not believe I was going off to boot camp, and every time I thought about everything that led up to this moment, from the time I swore in at MEPS until sitting in the airport chair, it made me shake my head and smile with pride and mild disbelief. I guess it was because growing up, I felt pushed down and held back, but now everything depended on me to make the right choices. I felt like I was about to fly like an American Eagle into the great unknown blue sky.

The announcement came to the board in the middle of our small talk. We hugged, and mom cried, and I made a funny face for dad's camera and to cheer mom up. Giving my seat ticket to the boarding assistant, I turned and waved, then boarded the plane for my trip to Chicago O'Hare International Airport.

The first thing I learned immediately was that no matter how tough I thought I was or how much knowledge I had acquired by studying and working out, I knew absolutely nothing about the military. After the plane ride from New Orleans to Chicago O'Hare, I grabbed my luggage, walked to meet the other eight people headed to training, and sat down at a coffee shop. It was about one in the morning, and I was dead tired and clueless about what was going on around me.

Suddenly, a man in uniform walked up to us out of nowhere. He was stealthily quiet and whispered in a monotone voice, "Let's go." He did not ask who we were or what we were waiting for. It was understood that if we were not in the right area of the airport to go with him, we would get left behind. Right away, we had to show initiative.

A few guys looked back, like they might take off in the other direction, but no one did. We just looked at each other wide-eyed, picked up our stuff, and quickly followed him to a white unmarked van outside the terminal. No one made a sound. I recognized him as a Naval petty officer from his uniform, or a non-commissioned officer (NCO) from my studying days in the NDEP, so I knew we were headed in the right direction.

We drove for what seemed like hours. The highway and back roads were icy, rough, and bumpy, causing him to drive slowly, moving through high snow drifts on each side. Were the powers that be trying to make it confusing to know where we were? In any case, they were doing a great job at it.

No one dared to sleep, and still no one made a peep. I just looked out the dark windows, waiting for my next steps of Navy bootcamp, or what I soon learned to be called the beloved " training evolutions." Finally, we arrived at recruit training. We drove through gate security, around a sharp bend, and up to the side of a building where two NCOs were waiting for us, and they meant business. I was instantly aware of the strict atmosphere and attention to detail they expected.

We quickly unloaded the van while the NCOs started yelling at us with the force of a hurricane. I swear someone started crying like a baby, and that was a bad mistake, gaining special attention from other NCOs in charge. They made him do push-ups until he learned not to cry, which took quite a while. I guessed that he would not survive boot camp and be administratively discharged due to mental incapacity to withstand the training.

We walked amidst the constant barrage of verbal attacks and screaming, shuffling, and scooting into the building. It was a freaking cold Illinois winter. And it did not help when we started sweating from the exercise games.

Other NCOs and a Chief Petty Officer (CPO) ordered us to put our stuff into a perfect line against the wall. We were rewarded with push-ups over and over for the next three hours until we got it right, creating a nice big pool of sweat on the ground. Welcome to boot camp, Navy Recruit Parr, you no-nothing, piece of crap.

We were thoroughly punished with all kinds of calisthenics and exercises until every bag was precisely placed, down to the very last millimeter between each one. After our first informal training, of learning how to put our bags in a line, we walked through other exercises of instruction, specially designed to immediately start breaking down our wills. This intense type of action registered with me, and I found that no matter what they did, I took it with a defiant grin and zeal, knowing they would not defeat me.

We were ordered to put our gear into a box to mail home, and made a phone call letting parents know we arrived safely. I had two minutes, and when mom heard yelling in the background, I just said it was part of the training. We said goodbye, and I hung up. It was time to get back to the fun.

Another CPO walked into the room and asked us if anyone could sing. What? I grew up in church singing in choirs and musicals, so I could carry a tune. I raised my hand and sang a measure of Amazing Grace, which was met with a nod, and was told to sit at a desk in another room.

Come to find out, I had been accepted into the Navy's elite unit consisting of a choir, band, and drill team. It was called Triple Threat, Company 909. Eventually, I found out why it was considered the elite company of which to be a part.

Next were urine tests, blood samples, physicals, and again a medical interview, while NCOs consistently helped us through very special versions of verbal reassurance to stand in lines one inch from the walls, and not talk. I had been up for over twenty-four hours by now, and started to feel it creeping into my brain like a hazy numbness. My whole body felt as if it were on autopilot, going through the motions with no thought about any of it. I just did what they said and when they said to do it, because I had no resistance to doing anything else.

The academic, psychological, and physical training, such as the impromptu screaming, academic tests, and extensive exercising, came surprisingly easy for me. I had experienced constant yelling working for dad when I screwed up in even the littlest of things, so I just smiled and shook it off. All of the physical evolutions experienced came easily because of bodybuilding.

Mentally, I felt freer than I had been in, well, forever, and the demeaning and condescending actions being done to all of us equally made me rethink all of the times it happened to me, or when I did it to myself. It was as if all the stuff I experienced had inadvertently trained and prepared me for this very experience. Had God allowed certain things to happen in my life to help me in these moments? Perhaps it was so.

Believe it or not, the toughest thing was trying to urinate into a tiny plastic cup, going into the second half of the second day with no sleep. When a hundred other guys are standing right behind you waiting to go, it gets very tricky. To your left and right, the same thing is happening. Recruits are so tired that they started to fall asleep going into the second day of processing, often missing the urine sample cup and peeing on other people's shoes. I am sure I peed all over someone's pants. Instructors were everywhere, even right between each urinal, looking down and up at us, yelling. They made sure we were peeing "correctly," and not on them. Like cowardly cattle waiting to use the bathroom two by two feet right next to each other, we were lined up and down a wide, long wall. With heads dropped to chins, each recruit slowly moved in a sleepy, drunken stupor.

A bunch of nervous and lethargic guys were trying to aim and complete their missions of peeing with several NCOs screaming at them to zip it up. Now, decades separated from these crazy days, I find myself laughing out loud and have absolutely no problem with using the public urinal. Once you have experienced what I did in boot camp, everything concerning this practice is a cakewalk.

Once medical was finished, we were commanded to walk single file without a sound to a room where we were assisted in getting bathroom supplies such as razors, shampoo, soap, and shaving cream. Next came our issued uniforms, including boots, coats, sweats, hats, socks, and other bootcamp equipment. Then we marched to our barracks and put it all away quickly, and it had to be perfect.

Again, we were given physical instructions to ensure we listened to every word that was spoken and the instructions given. Quickly, we started to execute orders the first time, every time. At the start of training, we had no idea how to organize our stuff, and the POs took this as an opportunity for impromptu recruit development.

We lined up in two rows like sheep in gates, moving

slowly forward, receiving multiple shots in each arm at once with this sort of air gun, then a giant one in the butt. It created a hard nodule of medicine in the backside that had to be worked into our muscles by pushing on it. We were laughing and groaning in pain from the butt shot, rolling around the floor, trying to get this hard, putty-like medicine absorbed into the muscle. It was funny and ridiculous at the same time.

The first several days were Processing Days (PD). Over the following weeks, my company had recruits come and go, whether through testing positive for drug use, lying about using them, health issues, or test disqualifications. We also received other recruits from other companies who rolled back into our unit. This time was built into our training to achieve the optimum number and quality of recruits for Navy classes, appropriate personnel, and accurate qualifications for both the rifle companies and the Triple Threat unit.

Haircuts that were more like scalpings were given during PD. A bunch of bald roll-on deodorant-looking newbies were going to get their lives wrecked and rebuilt, courtesy of Uncle Sam. Bootcamp was three months of beyond imagination and incredible transformations that eventually broke my will, but not my spirit.

Some recruits who flunked out of training stayed on the base and eventually went home, while others worked hard and were held back to eventually rejoin another company, but not me. This was my opportunity, decision, and future, and I did everything to make it exceptional. Nothing would stop me, no matter what.

Extreme physical punishment, surprise "Red Face" workouts, sleep deprivation, verbal exercises freely and generously given from the instructors and the company commanders were the order of the day. Extra training reminders that we were now in the Navy were commonplace, even when we did something right. Call it a warped sense of humor, if you will. And I loved every second of it.

Red Face drills occurred at all times of the night, sometimes throughout the night. These impromptu exercises were designed to force a quick mental and physical response of compliance, regardless of where we were or what we were doing. A mix of yelling, holding in a push-up position for hours, doing hot stoves until we threw up, and destroying our barracks, where everything we owned ended up on the floor, started to not faze us in the least. It is amazing what one can endure when a decision is made to defy the lies of defeat, physically, emotionally, and psychologically.

One evening, our company commander (CC) thought I was laughing too loudly while a few of us were standing around in the barracks discussing cleaning orders. He then commanded me to execute Physical Fitness Test Three, the last exercise evolution before graduation, which was not required for several more weeks. Right in front of him and his wife, who had just walked in with their baby, I dropped to the ground and pushed out my sets of pushups and sit-ups with ease.

I just assumed he wanted to show off to his wife, showing her he was creating some hard-charging, bullet-proof sailors who followed orders and did what was required, no matter what. When I finished, I requested to recover. He cracked a wry smile and nodded.

I popped up, saluted, and resumed my work in the barracks. Our CC had a warped sense of humor, and although he hammered us often, he was a great trainer and truly cared about his recruits. You had to like the guy, despite the crazy training and insane attitude he held.

Over the next twelve weeks, several of our fellow recruits were removed for additional specialized training, discipline, or discharged from the service. A few were sent to military prison for criminal activity. The company commanders also addressed those who needed concentrated physical fitness conditioning, who were overweight, or addressed administrative issues. We started with somewhere in the neighborhood of one hundred and forty recruits, and by the end of training, we finished with a little over half.

Everything I went through as a kid growing up had inadvertently helped me by forging a no-quit attitude and toughened me from the inside out to push through impossibilities, believing in God to help even when I did not see the help coming. I was a round peg in a round hole, and nothing could get to me.

Inspections to get our organization skills perfect were a daily occurrence, whether it was our lockers, beds, or uniforms. The tiniest detail missed, and we got punished harshly. We learned to be detail-oriented, and no excuses were accepted.

If our socks were not folded to exact specifications and positioned the correct way, including the lips of them, we paid the price of endless workouts. If underwear was not laid in our lockers just as the CC presented, we ran until our legs felt like they were falling off. The price of failing was very expensive, indeed.

I thought I was very good at details, no doubt from organizing and being obsessively perfect with my things over and over, starting as a very young boy. Being exact on my bunk, uniform, and barracks details, I was nominated and became the cadence caller halfway through training. This was the guy who stood outside the ranks to the side, singing to keep recruits in line and orderly during marches and runs.

However, I was removed a week later from that position for not being able to keep the stray strings off of my dungarees as I was instructed. If I could not make myself stay aligned, then I did not deserve to align others. As a leader, this was required, and I accepted my fate. It was the principle of it that mattered. No leader deserves to tell others what to do if he or she cannot set the example, with regard to leading others?

Being exact and dead-on with clothing and equipment was not in and of itself the requirement, but what it instilled in us as soldiers and future Naval seamen and airmen. These exercises were done to create a deep, involuntary conviction ever present, whatever the duty requirements. Whether on land, at sea, or on the ground, we were being taught to pay attention to the littlest things because this lack of attention to detail created larger problems if not addressed first and immediately, every time.

The choir, band, and drill team of 909 Triple Threat were required to practice as intensely and focus as any other part of military training. If we hit a wrong note, we were notified in ways that only boot camp could do. The drill team consisted of rifleman who trained relentlessly and practiced their routines over and over until they mastered those rifles. The band had to practice until every musician played as one solitary machine.

My CPO choir director stood in front of us, waiting to relay the order to assume pushup positions if we did not sing the right notes. It was all part of mastery, to keep us staying focused on the musical tasks at hand, learning how to sing in perfect tone and pitch. I had learned this even as a young boy when dad told us to dig a ditch, and had no choice but to do it right the first time, or get in trouble.

Unless someone has personally experienced this, it is a concept beyond familiarity. The Navy has a very specialized way of stripping one of their agendas, self-centered intentions, reflection of will, self-destructive attitudes, and a civilian mindset. This process strategically destroyed my individualistic promptings, erased my self-doubt and self-deprecating ways, creating a devout, patriotic team player focused at the deepest levels of my being.

I decided early on in training to make sure I was in incredible shape, always doing push-ups and sit-ups after classes and physical fitness training. Whatever the company commanders made me do, I was set on surpassing the physical fitness standards the US Navy expected of me to graduate from boot camp. Because of my outstanding physical standards and accomplishments, I was ordered to lead the company along with another friend who was going to be trained as a Navy SEAL. This is a highly trained group that operates in the sea, air, and land, anywhere in the world, and he was as tough as they get. My friend and I set the track pace in front of other companies at boot camp for the physical fitness test (PFT-3) before graduation, and set an outstanding record for the four-mile run.

Because I attended some college before joining the Navy, I was promoted twice at a small ceremony in front of fellow future bootcamp graduates in our barracks. This acknowledgement marked a significant achievement in the military before I even started my career as a sailor, and my college years turned out to be more useful than previously imagined. I call this one a God set up. I believe he provided these opportunities, and even though I did not finish my college, I was still rewarded for having attended.

On the day of our company's graduation, we marched into the giant World War II blimp hangar as the perfectly polished Triple Threat 909 Company. We performed at our boot camp graduation ceremony as the special entertainment. Included in the audience were special guests, parents, esteemed officers, civilians, and Very Important People (VIPs), including the Secretary of State, various generals from different branches of the military, and esteemed veterans from various wars. We knew what we had overcome, and we were soon to be recognized as United States Navy sailors.

My parents did not initially recognize me when my choir unit of Triple Threat marched up in formation, only five feet from where Mom and Dad were sitting in the bleachers, directly in front of them. When I started singing a solo in the song "Lean on Me," they recognized me and smiled proudly. I had another uncle who was in the army as a lieutenant colonel, sitting in the VIP section. The ceremony lasted for about three hours. Afterwards, everyone was invited to come down from the bleachers onto the deck of the hangar to hug and congratulate their loved ones.

After three months and two weeks of facing the hardest mental, physical, and academic training the Navy could throw at me so far, God transformed an insecure, unfocused, and undisciplined young man into a United States Navy sailor. No more did I have attention deficit issues, feelings of lingering insecurity, or lack self-worth and internal fortitude. I defied the lies of negative self-perception and was transformed from the inside out, now set mentally and physically to begin my next training evolution, technical training school.

Chapter 11:

NAVY SCHOLAR

Arriving at the Navy Air Technical Training Center (NATTC) Millington barracks in Millington, Tennessee, I walked through the front door, immediately sensing an element of pure seriousness. Several guys were burying their heads in books, like college students cramming for a final exam the next day. The atmosphere was more of a college dorm than the military, yet the lockers, bunk beds, and spotless interiors of the sleeping quarters were an immediate and constant reminder that I was in the Navy.

This step in training was considered to be less strenuous physically than boot camp, but discipline throughout was still expected. Since it was an advanced school preparing me for what I would be doing in the Navy, focus was narrowed to technical jargon, mechanical verbiage, and strategic intricacies of my future job as an Aircrew Survival Equipmentman. The challenge would come in the academic portion.

The morning after I arrived, I classed up with the marines and sailors that I would be going through PR "A" school with, ran a few miles, took a shower, and then attended new student orientation. Afterwards, I had some free time to iron uniforms and prepare mentally for the next day's training. Being excited and nervous, my class of seven talked about where they were from, why they decided to join the military, and where they wanted to be stationed.

In school, the Marines (Jarheads) and Navy (Squid) trained side by side through it all. Jarhead and Squid are the nicknames given to each other because of the high and tight haircuts of Marines, and the fact that Navy sailors swim in the ocean at one point or another in their military careers. These sacred names are respected by both branches, often stated when one branch was trying to academically outdo the other one, and made for a great competitive atmosphere.

Every morning we woke up before five a.m., regardless of how long it took us to iron out our uniforms, study, and get ready for the next day. We ran four and a half miles religiously, showered, and ate breakfast. Then, after straightening up the barracks, we prepped and went over to the technical school for training by seven o'clock.

The hybrid classroom consisted of hands-on instruction, textbooks, and tests. We were responsible for absorbing an unbelievable amount of information given in a very, very short period from the instructors, even if we had to stay up all night to study. During one of our hands-on training evolutions, we were learning about the fundamentals of an NB-8 personal parachute, a survival gear parachute for personnel aboard aircraft if the need arose for an emergency egress due to unforeseen critical systems failure. There were several access points where the thread was attached to the high-tensioned nylon cord, holding it inside the parachute deployment system until the nylon parachute itself was ready to be released via the pull handle at the side of the NB-8 exterior skin.

My future job as an aircrew survival equipment expert required me to optimally perform my job perfectly the first time, every time, no matter where I would be assigned shortly. This was a highly stressful and extensively rigorous training program designed to quickly weed out the lazy, inadequate, and ill-equipped. I approached the table where the parachute lay open, exposing the inner cavity.

The heavy nylon strings ran out and down from the inside, extending the entire length of the table with the chute attached to the end of the lines. Mind you, this was the very first packing exercise, and one would think that you would have a chance to get it right a few times after studying the night before. Nope.

After the PR1(Petty Officer First Class Parachute Rigger) showed us how to do it once, I approached the parachute pack and was told to begin. Attaching the string to the inside of the sewn-in loops was tedious and very intricate. Incidentally, PR1 stood in front of me as I started packing the parachute, making the whole thing even tougher as my mind started to forget what I had just learned the night before.

I knew these procedures from studying hours about it the previous evening, but missed how to properly turn the loops in to properly release the mechanism. When the class was complete with their exercise, PR1 walked up to my parachute pack and pulled on the cord. It did not release as indicated and instructed, and I immediately failed the packing exercise. The next one did not go well either, and at the end of the first day of PR technical school, my class grade was a whopping fifty-eight percent.

The instructor became enraged, looked sternly at me, and bluntly stated in front of my classmates, "If you do not pass the next packing evolution, you will flunk out of this school and be sent to the fleet to scrape barnacles off the sides of ships." The next packing evolution would begin with many more parachutes to master the very next day, immediately after the morning run. I was nervous to say the least.

I just stood there in front of the class, scared out of my mind. I stared at the instructor, not knowing what to say, other than, "Yes, Petty Officer." All of a sudden, all of the struggles to pass high school flooded back. My mind swirled, I was panicking, sweating, and could not catch my breath.

Well, no matter what, failing out of Navy technical school was not the outcome I wanted. That kind of thing was known to get back to the fleet and stay with you for your entire Navy career. I was in a state of complete mental and psychological loss. That evening, I was freaking out and called my mother.

Telling her what happened, she encouraged me and prayed that my mind would supernaturally absorb the information, that Jesus would heal me from fear and confusion about studying and execution, and nothing I had experienced before would hinder me. Honestly, being full of doubt, I did not know how this dire situation would work out. But I did believe in prayer, and said "Amen."

The next day, my class of seven future aircrew survival equipment men and women walked into the gigantic training facility. Several parachutes were laid out in a maze. This method of equipment placement and gear assimilation was zigzagging all around the interior of the building, ensuring a mental shakeup for the newbies during school. It was time to learn the next type of parachute procedures, types, and literature found inside the ballistic release seat that fighter pilots used and some still use today, and I was not looking forward to it.

A Marine gunnery sergeant walked up to us in full, perfectly pressed camouflage. He was full of motivational energy, excitement, and seemed overjoyed when he introduced himself. Gunny was to take over the class and lead us through the rest of the training. What? Mom had just prayed that things would click and everything would go smoother.

Gunny could not have been more than thirty years old, yet held a razor-sharp stance of confidence that had been developed through years of wartime leadership and training. He encouraged, instead of belittling, saw the potential in each Navy and Marine student, and never stopped pushing us until we realized it ourselves. He was a brilliantly exceptional Marine, having advanced quickly in rank due to his mastery of the PR military trade and Marine practices.

Gunny did see exposure to wartime and earned medals of commendation and honor that set him apart. In spite of being a very accomplished Marine who could have put his ego out front and dogged us every step of the way, he took the time to know us a bit before returning to our training. Do not get me wrong, he was a Marine through and through, expecting us to perform outstandingly at every training interval and test. But by truly helping us, especially me, it let me know that he was on my side, wanting me to excel.

I aced every method of packing, stitching, and placing the pins in the correct order, and presented a perfect packing solution in the next parachute test. Each procedure was methodically and precisely relayed. The information I was told and had seen in training manuals was vividly imprinted in my mind and was recalled perfectly. I stated the packing requirements back to the instructor, verbatim, when I was told to execute. Yeah, that was a freaking miracle.

Every step in technical school was extremely stressful, and it was a pass-or-fail junction. At that time, during what was called parachute rigging training, you had one chance to memorize the equipment the night before, and immediately pack the parachute the following morning. I am talking pages and pages of information to absorb like a sponge, and I aced this task.

If the procedures of packing were not exacting to standards according to strict regulation and methods, the special operators, airman, pilots, and civilians who would wear these parachutes would die. And someone would know what happened, because every single pack prepared was signed off by the final inspector and the PR who packed it.

School was no joke, and had the reputation of being a life-or-death training protocol from early in its inception. At one point, students were required to line up NB-8 personal parachutes and pick one to jump out of a plane. If it was packed correctly, they survived and passed the class. If the chute did not properly operate, they were killed by their hand. However, the same level of expectation and skill attainment was required because one could not immediately prove their competency.

The first stitching exercise to be mastered was learning a box stitch. This type of sewing stitch was fundamental in sewing lanyards, webbing, and many types of survival gear, and constructing bags for hauling equipment, just to name a few. These and other types of sewing applications were required to be mastered in a matter of only a few hours, including various sewing machines, repair, and inspection techniques.

As we moved through each piece and type of gear, my class attacked and mastered every single one. Life rafts, survival vests, explosive gear, and many other variants of aircraft and aircrew survival gear had to be learned perfectly. We even aced the fundamentals of the sewing portion.

At the end of our aircrew survival equipment technical training, my class shattered the long-standing academic record for the school that had not been surpassed in over five years. I was last in my class, but still held a ninety-seven grade point average. I am so very proud of our 96.01 cumulative grade point average record that stood undefeated for years. Our class picture and GPA were hung on the academic distinction wall, an example of determination, sacrifice, and sheer will.

God helped me overcome a lot of anxiety about school, fear of the unknown, and gave me direction through every step of PR "A" Technical School as I kicked my butt and did the work to make it happen. Technical school felt like a year of demanding, intense, and rigorous learning stuffed into twelve weeks of an academic training regimen. From there, I felt fully prepared to take on any survival or protective gear requirement the Navy could throw at me.

After training was completed, it was time for us to pick orders to which we would be assigned after graduation. Excited to be finished with training and looking forward to our next assignments, my class was escorted to a room with several petty officers. We sat down at desks in a more relaxed, yet still disciplined atmosphere.

In front of the room was a large dry-erase board with black scribbled writing. These were the assignments from all over the world that we were allowed to briefly glance at before returning to our seats.

Quickly scanning the board, I saw many different types of assignments at various duty stations. Some were aboard supply ships, battleships, frigates, and aircraft carriers. A few were also land-based. There was this other one, too, written towards the bottom of the board. It was foreign to me, having never heard about it from my Naval delayed entry program.

In block lettering was written the name "Antarctic Development Squadron Six (VXE-6), Point Mugu, California." I went back to my seat and stared at it, stupefied. I turned around and whispered to the petty officer standing against a file cabinet behind me, "What is VXE-6?"

I stayed quiet and watched as everyone took turns picking their duty stations, but no one picked the one I was curious about. The petty officer (PO) I spoke to behind me walked up, leaned over my right shoulder, and whispered, "It's your turn. If it's not gone, pick AntarcticDevronSix." I slowly stood up quietly, walked over to the board, and saw that VXE-6 had not been taken.

The fact that no one else seemed to help pick their assignments was odd, but it happened. I was also the last one to pick my duty station because I was last in my class, even though I had an A, and no one else picked one of the most treasured and rare jobs to see come up on the board. I chose it, and we were dismissed to prepare for our graduation ceremony, a small but sincere closure from all the weeks of very exhaustive technical training.

My class was acknowledged as having successfully and with distinction achieved the rank of Aircrew Survival Equipmentman. We said our goodbyes and separated to our appointed tasks. I packed up my stuff, received orders in the transfer office, and in a matter of a few hours was on the bus to the airport, the portal to the rest of my military life. I could not have accomplished anything academically over those last three months without help from God, much less achieving Navy scholar status. I was failing miserably, yet somehow my mind was supernaturally transformed from a mess of confusion and fear into one that could absorb and excel at every task, a sign that miracles happen even today.

Dr. Eric Shannon Parr

Chapter 12:

SCIENTIFIC SQUADRON

As the airport shuttle drove me towards the front security gate opening to the Naval Air Weapons Station (NAWS) base in Point Mugu, California, I saw an F-4 Phantom jet fighter mounted atop a huge concrete triangle with a long line of United States American flags behind it. Suddenly, pride swelled up inside of me, and I realized that I had made it. After all the freaking hard work and overcoming impossible obstacles, I was on my way. I just stared at this amazing plane as the van drove us through the base entrance.

Not being used by the Navy any longer as a main strategic fighter/bomber aircraft for decades in the fleet, some of the still-existing F-4 Phantoms were converted into automated targets used to test missiles at NAWS. The F-4 was an aircraft developed during the Vietnam era. Dad had worked on them during that time and told me all about this amazing plane. It was a sort of confirmation, seeing that the aircraft told me this was exactly where I was supposed to be.

I checked into the main base office and was assigned to temporary barracks until they could find a permanent room assignment for me. I walked into a large, empty room and, looking around, put my green duffel bag on the bed that contained my uniforms and everything I owned in the world. I went to the chow hall to grab some lunch, walked around the base a bit, visited the base store, then headed back to my room.

Turning around and facing the still-opened door to my room, I noticed it was eerily quiet. There were no sounds anywhere, even from rockets previously being tested, as I first drove through the base entrance. It seemed as if everything ceased all at once.

No aircraft were flying overhead. No military personnel were seen walking around in front of or occupying my barracks. Then, it happened.

After seven months of fast-paced boot camp and technical training experiences, I found myself completely alone in a new environment with no one to talk to or interact with. Suddenly, I started to panic, wondering what I was thinking, trying to be a Navy sailor. Then, every past negative thought imaginable rushed into my mind.

Stupid thoughts, like why did I choose to join the military, and why did I get myself into this, began hammering my mind. Man, I was genuinely freaking out because I had no idea what to do next. Everything in the military was regimented and spelled out for me up until this point, but this was a whole new, strange environment.

Then, a deep depression and panic hit me, making me

feel like I was drowning. In spite of everything I had accomplished and established within myself, I started to doubt. I sensed I was starting to lose it mentally.

I cried out, "God, I'm so depressed! What am I going to do!" My world started crashing in on me, and despite being surrounded by people on the base, I felt alone. Then, out of nowhere, a petty officer showed up in the doorway and told me to grab my stuff because I was being moved to another barracks. I dried my eyes, picked up my duffel bag, and followed him down the sidewalk to another building, praying he did not hear me.

Despite all the academic achievements, athletic abilities, military discipline, and established credibility early in my Naval career, I surprisingly still dealt with some level of anxiety, fear of the unknown, and depression. I decided all I needed to do was keep my head low, keep learning, and do what I needed to do. For the good of my fellow shipmates and the squadron, remaining professional and mission-driven was my priority.

After settling in, I walked to the Antarctic Development Squadron Six, part of the NAWS base. I met Petty Officer First Class (PR1), who was the senior petty officer over the parachute rigger shop. The first words out of her mouth were, "So, you're the hotshot out of PR 'A' school, huh?" I just nodded and said, "I guess so."

PR1 smiled, nodded, and we talked as she led me to the shop where everyone was getting the aircraft and aircrew extreme cold weather gear ready for flight engineers and pilots deploying to Antarctica and New Zealand. PR1 was an awesome beacon of strength and full of positivity, always encouraging her parachute riggers whenever she saw us having a tough day. It was her mission not only to support Antarctic exploration but to make sure her people could perform at the top of their game.

I arrived in August, and the entire squadron was set to deploy in September. It was crunch time to get the squadron ready, so it was all hands on deck in my PR shop, a naval acronym for the aircrew survival equipment department. We hustled to sew, repair, inspect, replace, put into service, pack, and create all sorts of extreme cold weather equipment and gear.

The innumerable types of equipment in our aircraft, and that which was worn by the aircrew, were designed to protect and help our pilots, aircrew, and aircraft survive in every inconceivable and unforeseen scenario of Antarctica. Over the next few weeks, I stood twelve-hour watches occasionally, worked twelve hours at night, and slept in between. In the military, sleep was a convenience, not a necessity.

During the deployment season from August to March, personnel alternated duty stations between Christchurch, New Zealand, and McMurdo Station, Antarctica.

Since I was a newbie, I would be first assigned to Antarctica, or the "Ice" as it was known to those who had been there before. This selection process provided a crash course in mission parameters and threw a person into the deep end of the mission's requirements, since the squadron performed its primary duties on the Ice.

I was psyched, and my mind was spinning as to what I would encounter on the vast, frozen continent. Over the next month, I was expediently yet thoroughly certified in many areas of maintenance, taking classes specific to the squadron's mission as it applied to my job. This process was called a workup, and was continuous to varying degrees throughout my service in the military, depending on where I was assigned, and the length of time I was assigned to any particular duty station.

A few of the many areas in which I had to get qualified included liquid oxygen systems, wing life raft systems, onboard emergency first aid kits for both helicopter and cargo aircraft, and interior cargo fireproofing. Additionally, concealment panels, audio and oxygen mechanics and gear, auxiliary power units, inspections, repairs, and specific and relative maintenance on the equipment in the six UH-1N helicopters and seven LC-130 aircraft were the responsibility of my PR shop. This list only grew, and required expert, ever-increasing knowledge of which I delivered.

Time flew by as I became certified and up to speed to be ready for deployment. And before I knew it, it was time to go. I packed my duffel bag with the required gear, arrived at the hangar on my departure date, and waited to board.

Most LC-130s had already left early for Antarctica and New Zealand with our helicopters loaded into their cargo holds. My aircraft taxi to the Ice had gear and personnel bringing up the rear, packed to the limit with several tons of equipment crates, various shop necessities, aircraft parts, and machinery. Additionally, miscellaneous scientific research gear, not including several pilots, copilots, flight engineers, and shop support personnel, was loaded and strapped down to help our scientific missions succeed with excellence.

We filed on board the multi-million dollar grey and orange ski-equipped aircraft, making our way down each side of the cargo hold. I took off my SV-2B survival vest, found my spot, and sat down on the webbed bench seating for the flight. With my big, stupid grin, I was about to embark on an adventure far beyond anything I had ever conceived.

White box lunches were given out to the officers, pilots, flight engineers, and sailors representing various shops at VXE-6. We buckled our webbing seat belts, the runway was cleared for us to take off, and the aircraft rumbled to life. That plane shook and shuddered with reverberation from four extremely powerful turbo-propped engines. Regardless of how much hearing protection we put on and in our ears, the low, bellowing engine noise was still deafening, shaking everything throughout that flying tin can.

Gaining speed quickly, we shot down the runway and lifted off in a steep climb as our journey to Antarctica began. Even with a full cargo load, passengers, and full of fuel, the Hercules aircraft could reach cruising altitude at about two thousand feet per minute, enough to safely clear the California mountain ranges facing the base. Soon, we leveled off to our cruising altitude of twenty-eight thousand feet.

Admittedly, it was pretty humbling to feel that aircraft power up and away with some of the greatest pilots in the world behind the wheel. A few of them were even within a few years of my age. Many of the older pilots and co-pilots had specifically transferred from fighter squadrons in the fleet and requested Antarctic duty because of the type of unique dangers, monumental challenges, and unforeseen obstacles pilots often faced on every single flying mission in VXE-6.

The trip to Antarctica was going to take about twenty-four hours with stops for food, rest, and fuel at Hawaii, Pago Pago or American Samoa, and briefly at Christchurch, New Zealand, where Antarctic prep would take place. In Hawaii, I had a few hours to burn, so a few friends and I went to Pearl Harbor. We saw many types of warships, battle cruisers, supply frigates, and an aircraft carrier or two. There were more ships in the bay than I could count. It made me very proud to be an American serving in the United States Navy.

When we arrived and unloaded on the runway at the Naval Antarctic research base in New Zealand, I went to get my Antarctic extreme cold weather gear issue. It was a huge warehouse setup with every kind of survival gear imaginable. They had coats, hats, scarves, boots, and everything in between to help one survive in the extreme and relentless Antarctic weather, specified for civilians, scientists, and the military. Green-colored clothing was for the military, and red and yellow were for the civilians and scientists, regardless of who worked where during the summer or winter months. We were also given insulated clothing, such as long johns and plastic white boots filled with some kind of air.

I asked what filled the inside of the high-tech footwear because of the valve on the side of each boot. The gear expert looked me in the eyes and sternly said, "I don't know." Hello, scientific confidentiality. These guys meant business.

I was also issued a very heavily insulated matching set of green gloves, pants with suspenders, a fur-lined hood, and specialized eyewear. These sunglasses were densely polarized because everything we looked at on the Ice could damage our eyes, even blind us.

Speaking of blinding, the uniquely frozen and snow-covered terrain created a reflective effect, every surface becoming a mirror prism, magnifying the sun. Scientists who study the sun's effects go to Antarctica because it is very strong there during the summer months. The ozone layer being thinnest at the poles, theoretically, gives scientists great access to solar effects and other types of practical and applicable research environments.

After my Antarctic equipment issue, I walked to the personnel station resembling a sort of baggage check-in at a commercial airport. Everyone from construction workers, plumbers, to deep water divers, the New Zealand military, scientists, United States military personnel, and other civilians who work in Antarctica year-round were waiting to be taken to the frozen continent. Personal and military issue gear I brought was weighed, tagged, checked in, and set aside for the loading department.

Before it was time to load up, everyone watched films, totalling about four hours' worth of footage, about the history and discovery of Antarctica, precautions, practices, and dangers to be aware of during flight, and how to be ready for the sheer shock of being exposed to a completely alien environment. At this point in deployment, this mysterious frozen tundra's winter season was turning into summer, but it was still very, very cold. Having a temperature several degrees below zero was very normal at the beginning of the summer season, and alien to anything I had ever heard about. Since the sun is always down during Antarctica's wintertime and constantly up during the state-side's equivalent of the fall, winter, and spring, there are no normal seasons due to the way Antarctica is exposed to the sun and how the Earth rotates on its axis. This meant no matter how our bodies acted or felt, or how one was used to sleeping back in California, it would take a few weeks to get used to the constant daylight. Not sleeping for a few days due to adjustments in sleep cycles and work parameters was normal, taking me over a week to start getting even a few hours of sleep at a time.

Because there is only about three inches of snowfall in Antarctica annually and practically no humidity, it is technically a desert. And what should you do in a desert? You drink lots of water, tons of it, even when you are not thirsty. During indoctrination at the pre-boarding, extensive briefings were delivered about living and working in Antarctica, helping to make sure every single individual operating on the Ice was safe, especially when it came to dehydration, sickness, and sun exposure.

If we felt queasy, lightheaded, or had a headache, we were told to drink water and immediately report to the medical clinic. This idea of staying hydrated was pounded into our heads constantly before I even boarded the plane back in California. The vastly reduced levels of humidity could quickly kill a person .

Chapter 13:

CHEATING DEATH

After several hours of safety and informational briefing, those who were assigned to Antarctica walked over to their appropriate aircraft and loaded up. Others assigned to Christchurch walked over to another part of the processing station and registered to start duty there. Before I knew it, we were loaded up in our LC-130, strapped down, and on our way to Antarctica.

The ambient temperature outside our state-of-the-art LC-130, ski-equipped aircraft, increased up to minus seventy degrees Fahrenheit while flying thousands of feet above the Antarctic continent. Flying in the frigid air at a ground speed of three hundred miles an hour with an average temperature of minus seventy-five degrees Fahrenheit, the wind chill increased significantly above minus one hundred and twenty degrees Fahrenheit. LC-130's fuselage, engines, skis, and wings were always exposed to these extreme temperatures during missions, and constant observation of all flight systems was a mandated practice, regardless of the length of flight time. Having flown several hours nonstop, now only a few hours from Antarctica, we were in this very unforgiving and extremely cold air.

Our highly trained flight engineers, flight crew, pilots, and co-pilots were constantly aware of the aircraft's performance during flights. Throughout their trips, they made it a habit to oversee aircraft systems checks, cargo status, personnel well-being, and survival gear checklists. Nothing was ever overlooked. The status of hydraulic systems, wiring, heating, ventilation, and air conditioning systems, electronics, and hydraulically controlled surfaces was constantly monitored.

The LC-130 Hercules aircraft were heavily outfitted, reinforced, and specifically designed to operate successfully in Antarctica, no matter what was thrown at them. One key modification was the introduction of three massive, multi-million-dollar skis equipped with Teflon coating on the bottom of them that aided in a smooth surface on which to land atop ice. They were located port, starboard, and on the front of the aircraft with wheels between them. Whether concrete runways in California, or ice and snow in Antarctica, hydraulic systems alternately raised and lowered the skis or wheels depending on the type of ground surface and condition.

As everyone was going through their checks, the aircrew noticed something on the aircraft's indicators. The front nose ski hydraulics malfunctioned, causing the ski to drop down at a forward bow low angle. Without a ski that could be raised back to the starting position, then lowered properly, landing on the ice runway at Williams

Field would be impossible, or at the very least, fairly catastrophic.

The ski had to be raised back up to reduce drag until landing was imminent. If somehow the ski did unfreeze from its bow-low position and rise back up against the fuselage but stick and did not lower, the plane would have to land by the rear skis first, then onto the broken front landing gear. Even if the front ski snapped back into place against the fuselage, there was no guarantee the tire would lower properly, and landing without a tire could be a horrible mistake.

The front ski was designed to be used for turning on the Ice runway to control steering. The pilots would also have diminished control over where we went, with the front rubber wheels slipping all over the ice. If this happened, it could become a bad day, to say the least.

If the hydraulic systems in the nose ski could not be engaged, the nose of the aircraft would be lifted, and the pilots would have to adjust for drag, or the resistance of the air pushing down against the top of the skis. However, upon landing, the ski would be frozen as it sat, tilted forward and pointing towards the ground. Essentially, the nose ski would become a mangled shovel, digging into the runway upon touchdown.

This malfunction could cause a pogo stick effect with the aircraft catapulted up and over onto its side or back. The nose ski could also rip off upon touchdown and tear through a wing, punch through the fuselage into the cockpit or cargo area, or several things we did not want to happen. Unless God intervened, there was no way of winning in any scenario presented.

As the loadmaster frequently looked through the belly porthole at the frozen, stiff front ski and wheels, we continued to fly for what seemed like an eternity. Checking and rechecking hydraulic systems, talking to the pilots about possible procedures, and discussing the pros and cons of cargo ejection were addressed. I was in a situation where this plane landing could go tragically wrong, and I could be killed along with my buddies. I was scared and nervous, but chose to brace myself mentally and spiritually.

As we all watched the crew monitor the situation, it was uncharacteristically peaceful. It was still nerve-racking and loud from the engines, but calm. Everyone seemed to settle down and accept the scenario upon us.

Whether it was muscle memory from military training or because they were scared stiff, no one made a sound. Despite being a bit freaked out, I chose to maintain military bearing and put my trust in God, because ultimately, He was the one in control and knew what was going to happen. Besides, if we did have to make an emergency landing or crash, we would deal with any scenario as it came.

After what seemed like several hours, a tremendously loud slam reverberated through the floor from the front of the aircraft, as if something hit us from underneath. The noise was so freaking loud that it could be easily heard above the engines, making everyone jump at the same time. The ski became unstuck somehow from its bow-low position, returning flush to the bow of the plane, and the wheels ended up nestled perfectly between the ski. Being that it was frozen bow low, and the amount of air forcing that ski down, this was unbelievable. The loadmaster just shook his head and said to us that the ski just slammed back into place, having no reasonable explanation.

You could feel the tangible release of tension in the air, and someone even broke out playing cards on the top of the cargo. The guys started talking about what we just endured and theorized why the ski malfunctioned and dropped in the first place. The fixed ski problem was a welcome feeling, but we were not out of the woods yet. That ski still had to drop properly with a working hydraulic mechanism, holding steady the several tons of aircraft and cargo to land and come to a full stop.

Getting to the flying threshold where prepping for landing was mandatory, we quickly put on our extreme cold weather survival gear and grabbed our bags, setting them aside in a location to quickly disembark. I assessed the LC-130 Hercules' interior survival and safety gear, ran through personal safety checks, buckled into my webbed bench seat, and waited for the landing. The loadmaster checked the cargo stability and the overall interior condition of the plane's systems and mechanical status accessible in the hold. I could feel the air inside the aircraft getting colder forty-five minutes before the landing. It was not because of mechanical failure, but to help get us acclimated to the incredibly harsh Antarctic temperatures and environment described to us during the initial briefing.

As the LC-130 Hercules began its gradual descent, the pilots lowered the skis; first the rear two, then the front. Miraculously, the front nose ski stayed extended, and we landed safely on the glacial ice runway at Williams Field. We overcame adversity and faced possible death as a team, and our crew did an outstanding job at not giving us a fateful outcome. God was certainly watching out for us, making sure all was well.

The average temperature of Antarctica's summer, where it was daylight twenty-four hours a day, seven days a week, was around minus twenty degrees Fahrenheit with no wind blowing. Add a little hundred miles an hour wind whipping up a snow storm called a "Herbie," and the wind chill fell well below minus eighty degrees Fahrenheit. We began operations during Antarctica's summer, yet it was still freezing cold.

I took a picture out of the small, round port window just before the aircraft came to a full stop and unloaded at Williams Field. As I walked down the ladder, putting my first foot down onto the thousand-year-old icy glacier, the sheer freezing temperature was not what I expected; it was much worse. It was also unrealistically bright, this alien world being nothing I had ever seen before. The sheer sub-freezing temperatures shocked me badly, causing me to slow my breathing and take in air gradually, so my lungs could adjust and not freeze.

It felt like I was hit square in the face with a frozen brick that stayed on my face, and never melted. Looking around through my specially polarized sunglasses at the frozen snow and ice mountain ranges, valleys, and frozen sea took my breath away. I was standing on thirty-five feet of compacted snow and ice atop eighteen hundred feet of water. The cold was so harsh and immediate that it penetrated my extreme cold-weather gear and seeped into my bones.

Many types of buildings lined the front part of the runway, built and anchored to the ice. Colored orange, green, yellow, and grey wooden and metal buildings contained all manner of equipment and supplies to keep the snow off the runway. A few buildings housed the maintenance crew that maintained the runway and aircraft before, during, and after takeoffs and landings in ideal landing and takeoff conditions. Still, others contained survival bags and equipment.

We walked over to the Nodwell, a large and very tall red vehicle having gigantic tires used as a people mover, and loaded up. We stared out of the windows in reverential silence, unable to speak, if only in hushed tones. The inside of the people mover was like being inside a huge rolling freezer.

I was glad to have my survival gear on, to say the least. Our mega traveler was outfitted and designed to operate on the Antarctic landscapes and had been proven to be effective through the decades. We were taken to the

Navy's scientific research station, McMurdo Station, Antarctica. At the administration building, we received important mission information. I received a haircut, ate something, and went to the barracks.

My sleeping quarters were right out of the 1950s, complete with twin bunk beds, green shaggy carpet, and old pine panelboard. Understandably, this was the early 1990s, and sleeping aesthetics were not as important as blatant survival in Antarctica. I wondered what lay ahead for this Antarctic newbie in this frigid, foreign landscape.

Dr. Eric Shannon Parr

Chapter 14:

SURVIVE OR DIE

After arriving in Antarctica for the 1992-1993 deployment, I spent the next two days getting acquainted with the base before leaving for Antarctic Survival School. I checked out the supply store, the location of my PR shop, where I would be sleeping, the recreational areas, and other buildings. It was an eye-opening adventure, even at this early point in my deployment, that I never would have imagined.

Not only did the base have top-secret experimental equipment that I had no idea what it was, but there were also scientists, scientific laboratories, and civilians walking back and forth. There were buildings for water desalination, storage tanks, equipment buildings, parts depots, petroleum tanks, and everything in between. This place was a thriving, scientific community that from the outside looked like a bunch of metal, wood, and crudely built structures.

Inside, they were heavily reinforced shelters designed to withstand the freakishly harsh snowstorms and freezing weather that could change at the drop of a hat. Some even contained gyms, coffee shops, and state-of-the-art luxuries, a must in the middle of this most remote naval base. The interiors were built for ease, and the exteriors for withstanding the harsh elements.

Indeed, Antarctica is the most unforgiving and mysterious continent on all planet Earth. Storms with blowing winds exceeding a hundred miles an hour turned ice and snow into thousands of slicing and sanding shards, decimating and freezing solid any piece of exposed skin within a few minutes. Towards mid-season of scientific research, development, and support missions, snow starts to melt in downtown McMurdo, quickly covered with snow whenever storms pop up.

The sheer cold causes frostbite on an uncovered ear or finger in a very short time, even in the early summer frigid temperatures. Embracing unimaginable Antarctic dangers and learning how to stay alive was what Antarctic Survival School was all about, and I could not wait to go. Having unpacked my stuff and now relaxing in the main sitting area of the multi-level barracks, one of the petty officers yelled out my name, telling me to pack for survival school.

I grabbed my gear and quickly ran out the door towards a giant vehicle parked in the middle of two buildings next to where I was staying. I met others who also had no survival training, and for whom this was required. We carefully made our way up four ice-laden, steel corrugated steps into the back of the cross-country vehicle named the Nodwell, after Bruce Nodwell, a Canadian inventor.

The ten-foot-tall vehicle lurched abruptly forward and, slowly, gradually began to move. It was a gigantic box on top of lifted tank tracks without any kind of suspension. There were seven small rectangular windows on each side of the passenger compartment, and two on the back doors where we boarded, packed in like sardines. The cab where a few drivers were sitting was separate from the personnel area, directly in front.

Most trainees sat on tiny metal benches extending down each side, and others had to stand. This giant people mover was designed and built for crossing extreme terrain, but no one considered comfort, second only to survivability. If this crawling, mechanical Goliath had enough fuel in its gigantic tanks, I was sure it could travel anywhere across this vast, frozen landscape.

All kinds of questions ran through my brain. What the heck was I in for? Why did I have to do this thing so early into my first deployment? Why could I not just get acclimated to my surroundings first before all of this?

After creeping along the Antarctic tundra for miles, we arrived at the remote field training site and facility of Antarctic Survival School. I grabbed my gear and carefully stepped out of the back of the vehicle, down the stairs, and onto the frozen Ross Sea.

Everywhere I looked was a thousand miles of frozen water, glaciers, ice ridges, snow, and gigantic Antarctic mountain ranges. We dumped our gear into a large pile on the frozen snow and went to the I-Hut, or instruction hut, for book and verbal instructions on how to stay alive during "Happy Camper School." This program was fondly given that name by previous attendees decades earlier. Over the next two-and-a-half-day course, I would get to know exactly what I would encounter, what to expect, and how to adapt and overcome. I entered the surprisingly large, half-domed rectangular training hut with the others who were there to both instruct and train.

The training building had been recently exposed to a heavy storm and was partially covered with snow and ice, with only the top third of it peeking out. The wood, canvas, metal-framed, and rope-reinforced structure appeared stronger than it looked. There was a tool shed with saws, shovels, pick axes, and mechanical tools to the side of it, used for camp instruction and survival.

Inside the I-Hut was pretty warm, courtesy of the primitive wood-burning stove. I found myself looking forward to getting back into the cold briefing before the teaching even began. We learned about getting burned by the sun, both on our skin and in the eyes.

This was very important because reflective white surfaces were obviously everywhere we walked, and not putting on the appropriate one-hundred percent UVA protective goggles resulted in "snow blindness," called photokeratitis. Wind blistering was a possibility when the skin was exposed, chaffing rapidly, mimicking the superficial epidermis damage of getting sunburned. Instructors also educated us about other types of skin damage, such as the causes of frostbite, what it looked like, and how to treat it. If frostbite occurred after prolonged exposure to the harsh Antarctic elements, as it had in the recent past with other crews who stayed in Antarctica, time would be of the essence as the degrees of frostbite progressed.

A waxy, red or white in color skin texture indicated frost nip, the first sign. Second through the fourth degree indicated hardened skin to black, stiff tissue, and eventually having the muscles, tendons, and ligaments permanently damaged. This is complete tissue loss. Once this occurs, amputation is mandatory to prevent infection spreading to the heart, resulting in certain death.

Hypothermia was emphasized as being more common in people who worked and lived in Antarctica than we realized. We were instructed to always watch out for each other and note any out-of-the-ordinary behaviors signifying the development of this very dangerous condition. Mumbling, stumbling, groaning, incoherence, and tumbling onto the ground while losing one's footing could all be signs.

Extreme shivering that stopped suddenly was an immediate indication of a person's core temperature not self-regulating and dropping, resulting in a person's death. We also learned about Herbie Alley, where very strong snowstorms called "Herbies" came from the south and produced winds over a hundred and forty miles an hour. These were fast and furious, remaining for hours or a short time, leaving just as mysteriously as they arrived. There was no way of predicting them. If the aircraft was grounded because of these storms, it was called having a case of the "Herbies, and the aircraft pilots, crew, and ground support adjusted missions accordingly.

Highly trained instructors covered different types of methodology concerning radio transmissions, and how to operate high-frequency (HF) and ultra-high frequency (UHF) settings with handheld and stationary radio sets. Learning how to use all of your senses while walking or hiking in white-out scenarios, especially when a storm rose, completely blocking anything to see, was paramount. Tents, igloos, gear, and other personnel two feet from you would be completely invisible. After the verbal training segment, we left the hot instructing hut, loaded up into our Nodwell tracks vehicle, and headed out further onto the Ross Sea frozen surface for hands-on, practical survival instruction.

As I walked out of the mover onto the frozen sea, I happened to look up and to the right, stopping in sheer awe. To this day, this gigantic white mountain of snow, ice, and rock previously covered by the clouded sky stood in full view, and was the most incredible thing I have ever seen. I later learned it was Mt. Erebus, a fully active volcano.

The twelve thousand, four hundred foot monster is the second largest known volcanic mountain in Antarctica, and is always puffing smoke from fiery hot magma deep in its belly. If that sucker ever stopped completely emitting smoke, pressure builds, and a gigantic eruption may be imminent. If this happens, it could theoretically produce enough power and force to cause a major geographical altering event. The clarity and reflective properties of the snow and ice seemingly reduced visual distance, making everything closer than it was, including Mt. Erebus. From our survival school location, it was over twenty miles away, but it did not look further than five. Taking in the vast, pure white environment of Antarctica was all the more unbelievable, and humbled me to the core.

To help keep everyone in my group from overexposure, avoiding impromptu, immediate weather hazards and storms, and to make a place for stoves and survival gear, everyone pitched in and built a snow and ice wall with base ledges. Some were assigned the task of sawing solid, frozen snow blocks and ice from the frozen sea floor. Getting these materials was an arduous and tiring task that was extremely taxing and used for other types of shelters. During the build, some of the team hauled our equipment closer to our survival site, while others helped to begin necessary survival projects.

One of the oversized ice saws, twice the size of a typical wood saw with large double serrated teeth, made short work of cutting out the ice floor. I used it to chew up and section the ice into two-foot by one-foot blocks. It took the entire team several hours to produce roughly eighty ice blocks measuring two feet by one foot by one foot. We used them, using snow as mortar to fill in the cracks, to build our initial structure.

The snow quickly hardened in a matter of minutes, creating a large wind barrier. When we finished, it did an excellent job of keeping out the crosswinds and helped to keep us a little warmer. I could not believe how effective it was, both as a cold barrier and wind deflector. After completing the wind wall, I put down my pickaxe and helped open up other survival gear.

Setting up the stove quickly was paramount. Getting some kind of warmth into our bodies helped our core temperature and gave us a feeling of security and well-being. We cranked up the portable gas stove and put snow into a pot for melting to make hot chocolate. My small cup of cocoa may as well have cost a million bucks. I lifted that small mug of deliciousness to my freezing lips without my gloves, daring the cold to attack, and swallowed it down with almost a single gulp. Life could not have been better.

The survival school participants included a Lieutenant Commander, a Lieutenant, enlisted men and women, and a few civilians who were scientists and survival expert trainers. All had smiles of accomplishment and were talking about our next training evolution. We drank our steamy goodness and ate granola bars with fatigued but satisfied faces. I cannot explain completely the feeling of accomplishment I had, but from how each person congratulated the other, we all felt the same way. Besides, in this environment, there was no time for formalities, only sheer survival, and we defeated this training obstacle together.

Our instructor told us to rest up for a few minutes, making sure we were bundled up correctly because we were going to receive an in-depth course on building other kinds of survival shelters. Additionally, the standing orders were to stay vigilant, watch out for signs of health changes, and note any changes in terrain formation, such as cracks in the sea floor. We were also on high alert for any Herbies creeping our way. Our instructor gave simple and exact instructions. Build the shelters wrong, and freeze to death. Forget a piece of extreme cold survival gear, say a glove liner or even long johns, and eventually lose a finger or leg. Basically, be prepared to freeze in your sleep if you fail to remember certain survival criteria.

It was very easy to build a shelter, thinking our bodies were okay because we were moving all the time. However, sweating is a constant, even when it is beyond freezing, and one's core temperature can fluctuate because the water pooling onto one's body evaporates, drawing heat away. The core temperature of a person can get so low that shivering ensues, where the body tries to warm itself up.

If the temperature drops too low and one ignores this fact, then hypothermia might result, as instructed inside the I-Hut. If we did not make sure we were ensuring proper clothes layering practices taught to us, death may ensue. Many, many details had to be quickly absorbed and applied, just like in PR "A" technical school, ensuring better chances of survival.

Herbie snowstorms popped up in the mountains' corridors. This, inevitably, happened at the worst times and in the least popular ways. If we did not sufficiently build the assigned snow shelters well enough, fatal exposure gave way to becoming human popsicles, stuck in the middle of a negative seventy-five degree below zero Herbie storm, freezing solid in our clothing,

The team decided to divide and conquer to make building the various types of other shelters more efficient. One of them was a sort of recessed lean-to trench, jokingly called a "shallow grave." Its walls came from the frozen snow floor covering the surface of the sea. These thin rectangles were leaned against each other over a survival trench, dug into the thick, frozen snow.

The sizes of these snow blocks measured about three feet long by two feet tall by eight inches thick. The way the blocks were created allowed a slight increase in temperature inside the ice shelter. The trench, about three feet deep, happened to be shoulder width for the person who volunteered to stay in it to sleep, but it can vary slightly from structure to structure. Building the shelter with the closed end towards the downwind direction helped to keep the person as warm as possible.

Because the shelter was open at one end, this sort of survival shelter was designed to be built quickly to prevent exposure to emergencies, especially if a fast-moving storm was approaching. A person had a better chance of not getting covered up in snow once the storm hit with this build. It was not a permanent solution for long-term survival, but it was absolutely necessary to stay alive until help arrived or the environment changed. For long-term survival, there was the frozen snow shelter.

Aside from the equipment already stationed at the makeshift kitchen inside the perimeter of the ice wall we first created, we took the backpacks and surplus extreme cold weather equipment and made a huge pile. Then we threw a ton of snow on top of our gear. Using our shovels to pack it down as much as possible, we kept repeating the process. In twenty minutes, we had a large enough pile to make a pretty good-sized shelter.

While throwing shovel after shovel of snow, we talked about adventures so far, goofing around, and making the best of a frozen situation. We constantly messed with each other, saying who would be the first one to have a toe fall off or finger turn black. Braving and facing the world's most unforgiving elements out in the middle of nowhere, we quickly became a close team helping each other out, even if it meant making tasteless jokes to get through the hardships.

The snow piled up was soon frozen solid, standing about five feet tall, ten feet wide, and fifteen feet long in an irregular rectangle. A three-by-three-foot square hole for an entryway was dug out at one end of the frozen pile, gaining access to where the gear lay. Slowly and steadily, we took turns entering it, removing the backpacks, and scraping out the inside until we had a nice frozen snow roof. Once finished, it was surprisingly roomy. We dug the floor down a bit with a shovel and an ice saw to make it easier to crawl inside.

After the shelter debrief following our build completion, four of us crawled inside the frozen snow shelter. We immediately realized it was warmer than the exterior climate temperature by over twenty degrees. All I cared about was not becoming a human block of ice while sleeping.

Shedding my overstuffed coat, hat, gloves, and boots, I crawled into my sleeping bag, zipped it up, and looked up at the glowing icy-blue ceiling from the sunlight barely getting through. I just stared in amazement at this solar wonder, falling quickly into a well-deserved sleep.

The absence of humidity played crazy tricks on my body, making my skin feel like 200-grit sandpaper. After a few hours, I awoke feeling very heavy as if weighted sheets were holding me down, and I moved very slowly. And I was thirstier than at any time I could remember.   It had to be because I was already dehydrated after only being in Antarctica for a few days. I was thoroughly forewarned that it would be like being on another planet. Incidentally, that dried-out feeling never completely left me the entire time on the Ice, regardless of how much water I drank, for both of my deployments. I crawled out of the snow igloo and was met with a feeling of a frozen snowball glued to my head.

We did our thing in the snow toilet outside, marked by a yellow flag, helped pack up the yellow field tent, and secured the rest of the gear. From enlisted to officer, we equally helped to pack up the site and get it ready for the next series of Happy Camper training. We pre-packed for departure, then assembled by our ice windbreaker wall for some breakfast consisting of Meals Ready to Eat (MREs).

After cleaning up from eating, we were instructed on the next evolution of training: glacier and ice crevassing.

Breaking up into a few parties with each one having a few guides, we headed out onto a gigantic glacier pass. Civilian experts made sure we had a fighting chance to pass this part of the Antarctic school course without killing ourselves. Roped together, we walked either side by side or right in front of the other, depending on the exercise, gradient, difficulty, and complexity of terrain.

There was no room for error, slowly moving forward, gently poking around the frozen, uncertain ground with our hiking sticks. Walking along the deceitful terrain using our peripheral vision, we slowly made our way up a long, icy incline covered with a thin layer of white powder. Digging our boots into the icy landscape when the gradient increased, we had to be very careful not to step on any fissures hidden beneath the snow-covered glacier.

These cracks could easily have opened up and revealed a giant eight-hundred-foot or deeper crevasse, swallowing alive the entire hiking party, and no one would know where we were. Falling several feet onto jagged ice, rocks, or into a narrow edge could result in crushing us. Yelling for help could never work because snow and ice are an incredible sound isolator.

It was not uncommon for people and equipment to be swallowed up inside these gigantic, secretive ice cracks. This has happened more often than not down through the decades of Antarctic exploration, no matter how carefully or expertly people are trained. Needless to say, it was most necessary to stay on the defensive and be keenly aware of everything around us.

As we hiked, the guide suddenly yelled out for us to stop and look down, showing us one of these hidden fissures. I was just a foot or so from it, but I might as well have been standing right on top. Shaking in fear, I slowly put my hiking staff into the crack, carefully walked over it, and kept moving forward. Thankfully, we were tied together, so if one person happened to fall into a crevasse, the others could try to dig their ice axe into the glacier before more fell in. Talk about walking on frozen eggshells.

Despite the ever-present dangers, we did what we were required to do despite feelings of fear, never thinking of what could be, and constantly staying present and aware. Dwelling on dying was not an option; only completing the mission, even during practice evolutions. The crazy thing was that you did not know how wide the crevasse was, cleverly covered up by frozen snow until it cracked open without warning.

We also learned how to arrest ourselves. If you suddenly found yourself sliding down an icy incline, you had to flip onto your stomach while falling. Swinging your ice axe and digging it into the ice or frozen snow to your side, above your head, or by your legs, depending on how and where it broke, helped to stop the horrific result of sliding off the edge of a glacier, iceberg, or ice wall.

After hiking through the tundra, performing other survival tasks, and going over essential equipment, we were given a camp debrief, then ordered to pack up and load the Nodwell personnel carrier. Having an extensive academic, hands-on, and exhaustive safety and technical training in every area of Antarctic survival, the odds of staying alive in this elite scientific community for my country increased exponentially. The corporate sense of accomplishment was immense. My group successfully graduated from Happy Camper School, and I will never forget these unreal adventures.

Defying the Lies: A Memoir

Dr. Eric Shannon Parr

Chapter 15:

MONSTER ICE TRUCK

My first job on the Antarctic continent was to work in the duty office. It was called the duty office because appointed Navy personnel were required to stand duty, keeping watch over the takeoffs and landings of our aircraft. Every enlisted newbie paid their dues and worked there as part of the initiation for being their first time on the Ice.

The room was composed of faded green walls, an old fan in the corner, two metal desks, and two chairs. It also had rudimentary maps, an old computer with a keyboard, a corded phone, geographical texts, and a white dry-erase board. My primary responsibility was to keep track of the LC-130 aircraft leaving and arriving on the Williams Field ice runway.

Every time an aircraft took off or landed, the rotary dial phone with the long, green coiled cord rang, and air traffic control notified the duty office of aircraft activity. There was another person in the duty office who answered the phone, and I wrote down the information, including the tail number and takeoff time, copying it onto the whiteboard. After each mission was completed, I wrote down the landing time and again the plane's tail number.

To have tunes, I brought my radio into the office to play cassette tapes and to catch whatever the local Antarctic radio station was playing. The powers that be did not care, giving me some sort of civility in the middle of nowhere. I bought that Sony boom box on base at the Navy exchange before deployment, and that thing lasted for years after the military.

In the duty office, I had the awesome privilege of driving these gigantic Ford vans converted to something that resembled monster trucks. They were used to transport people to and from Williams Field and around the base. The entire drivetrain had been replaced with off-road gearboxes and reinforced with heavy-duty frames. Forty-inch off-road tires with the van's ride clearance height of three feet helped to keep the Ford monsters from getting stuck in the snow, ice, and cracks in roads and the ice runway.

The road I drove on ran along the edge of the land mass adjacent to the Navy base, and dumped onto miles of thick, frozen sea ice where it went out to the glacier runway. This road from McMurdo Station to Williams Field was the only way to bring arriving and departing crews, personnel, and very important persons (VIPs). It was created every season, and although prepared with the best of accuracy and forethought, the road seemed to have a mind of its own on any given day, showing cracks and stress marks.

Even when marked out on either side with stakes driven securely into the ice with orange flags attached to the tops of them, the road occasionally disappeared at the drop of a hat. Often, the road visibility dropped to zero, lost in the blowing ice and snow. Let me tell you, there was more than one time I was glad to have these orange indicators on each side. I did not want to get stuck on the Ross Sea and have to wait out the weather.

Before every drive to the field, I went through the checklist of what to do and what not to do with the duty vehicle. One specific necessity was to make sure the truck had been plugged into an electrical outlet the night before. Our mechanics devised a way to attach an electrical cord to the truck's engine with a regular cord plug on one end to keep the oil from freezing and cracking the engine block.

Otherwise, it froze due to broken or brittle wires, plastic fittings, or snapped metal mechanical parts. The crazy low temperatures could freeze an engine solid, radiator and all. Needless to say, our mechanic shop in Antarctica had its hands full.

One morning, on a beautiful, clear day without a cloud in the sky, I had to go and pick up some VIPs down at the runway for my first drive of the day. I went through the pre-drive checklist and made sure the block was unplugged. I started up the rig and still marveled at how quiet it was outside, despite the roaring sounds of the truck. Snow is indeed nature's soundproofing.

I felt a bit invincible behind the wheel of that giant rig, but held strong to the belief that I was not beyond incident at any given point throughout my long deployment. It was still terribly cold outside, the thermometer registering at thirty below zero, with the wind slightly blowing. The monster orange Ford felt like a deep freeze on the inside, even with the heater blasting inside the sparse cab. With all of my extreme cold-weather gear, I was still very cold. I slowly drove past the churning desalination plant, reinforced helicopter pads, giant grey oil tanks, and several scientific buildings and equipment.

It took several minutes to drive away from the scientific base and to the outer banks. I approached the frozen sea and told myself with some reserve that everything was going to be okay. The snow-covered bluish ice would either hold the weight of the truck, or a crack might open up and swallow me and the van whole.

It was what it was. I came to the edge of where the land mass met the sea, now a passageway of caution and unknowns, as told to me during the Antarctic driving safety briefing. Slowly, I let off the brake and depressed the accelerator. The huge gears underneath, designed to make the wheels and tires climb over and across anything, crept the truck slowly forward. Down the man-made ramp carved out of the rock and gravel land edge, I drove. Holding my breath in anxiety, I eased the front, then the rear of the truck forward even more until all four wheels settled onto the frozen sea ice.

I firmly stopped with my foot on the brake and just took in the unbelievable place in which I found myself. Letting out a huge sigh of anxiety, I released the tight brake, and the modified truck, geared so low and powered so high, lurched forward by itself. The giant rubber and steel wheels began rolling slowly on the ice road as I kept the orange flags located on either side of the road in my sights, making my way to the distant runway.

At ten miles an hour, it took a long while before arriving at the Williams Field. Pulling around to the designated loading zone, I picked up the Admiral of McMurdo Station and another crew that had just landed the aircraft. They quickly threw their survival gear into the van, loaded up, and buckled down.

I nervously and slowly turned around in my seat to make sure everyone was secured. I was told before leaving the base that I would have the Admiral in my van, but I was still sweating bullets. I felt as if every time I made the slightest move in my seat, I was being visually scrutinized. I checked my weather through the front windshield, noticing the sky was clouded up significantly, but I felt we could get to the base before any bad weather hit us.

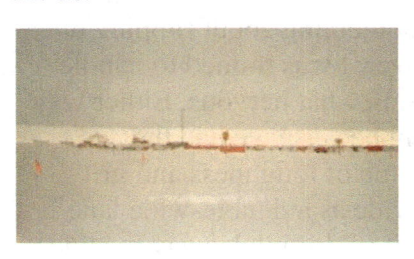

I asked if the esteemed Admiral and the crew were good to go. He looked squarely at me, smiled, gave me a nod, and that was my cue to get them base side. I started driving back when, out of nowhere, that storm I thought would not show up, did. And it came with a vengeance.

The winds became rough enough to completely erase my visual of the road, and skewed my vision of where the road ended and the sea ice began. Sensing my passengers were a bit shaken up, I slowed down even more and looked back to assure everyone it was going to be okay. Truthfully, I was trying to convince myself the most.

My eyes darted back and forth on the road, trying to pick out any cracks or gouges that may have opened up or obstacles that could be blown onto the road. The orange flags, attached to the tops of the spikes hammered into the ice, whipped all over the place. The shoulder of the road was supposed to be apparent, but the farther I drove, the more the indicators disappeared and reappeared, even though they were only just a few feet from me. It was like driving at night without your lights, but instead of complete darkness where the sky had no visible stars for reference points, the white, snowy sky blended into the icy road surface.

Now, the van started shaking side to side wildly with each gust of snow and ice, slamming violently against the sides of the truck. It did not help that the vehicle had huge lifted springs either, making it top-heavy. I sensed my passengers were wondering what was going on outside the van, muttering something about flipping over. Honestly, if it had flipped over, I was trained to handle the situation even if I felt somewhat nervous. Either way, we would weather this storm because we had the Antarctic Admiral, the epitome of toughness and grit.

The road was about as wide as a double-wide lane in the States, so it gave me a bit of driving leeway to slide when the winds aggressively pushed me. As I looked ahead, the sky still seemed to touch the ground. The storm lasted most of the trip, but as soon as I placed the front two wheels onto McMurdo Station, the storm disappeared. While focused on coming out the other side of this Herbie, I remembered that our fearless pilots normally flew in this crazy weather, regardless of how bad it was, so I wanted them to know I was capable. Not being able to see the runway more often than not, our LC-130 pilots and aircrew relied heavily on the aircraft's instruments to know how far the runway was from the skis, right before they landed. It was more normal than not for our pilots to land using only instruments in negative visibility conditions during mission completion. And I had utmost respect for those men and women of steel nerves and grit. My fortitude was not as tough as theirs, but I was doing my best.

After what seemed like over an hour, the winds stopped, and we made it back to McMurdo. I dropped everyone off at the large multi-story administration building, drove back to the duty office, did my mechanical checks after completing the run, and plugged in the engine block. This sort of adventure was repeated several times before my requirement in the duty station was completed.

I constantly utilized skills acquired and knowledge gained through my Antarctic safety training during this first deployment. I will forever have a deep respect and appreciation for Antarctica and all its wonder, danger, and largely undiscovered country. Undoubtedly, this mysteriously beautiful continent is a creative masterpiece that God truly loves.

Chapter 16:

PLACE IN THIS WORLD

My second deployment to Antarctica was much different from the first. I was allowed to work in the aircrew survival equipment building, for which I was trained. We constantly worked on cold-weather survival sleds, emergency rations, flares, flight suits, explosives, helmets, audio equipment, and other types of gear. Life was always busy, and there was something to accomplish every single day.

We worked at least twelve-hour shifts inspecting, repairing, and maintaining all of the extreme cold weather prototype and standard issue clothing, flight, and survival gear. My responsibility was to make sure both the aircraft and aircrew were ready to face, perform, and overcome in the midst of any type of survival scenario during their missions, every single time. Perfection in executing one's duty right the first time, every time, was still the standing order, no matter what.

Mandatory and necessary duty requirements had great potential to create stress and burnout while maintaining the highest level of gear preparation, squadron performance, and mission completion. I was relieved to know that there were some sort of modern conveniences to relieve distress, and we did our best to have a positive work-life balance. Having stress release and relaxation through these intense times helped to keep my mind on an even keel, and kidding around in the midst of maintaining perfect squadron performance was not beyond the norm in my shop, even while waxing floors.

There were three gyms, two for weightlifting, and a third for treadmills and overall cardiovascular health, all of which became my second home. My favorite coffee shop, once a designated officer's club, was available to play games, get a slamming cappuccino, and visit with other McMurdo workers from all walks of life. We even celebrated Thanksgiving and Christmas with fellow shipmates and invited civilians. During the Christmas holiday, the helicopter hangar became Santa's house. Reminiscent of the Woodstock concerts in the 1960s but not as crazy as they were, the civilian workers played their hearts out on a trailer converted to a stage, jamming to familiar tunes, original music, and music requests.

During my second deployment to Antarctica, I prepared a song by Michael W. Smith entitled "Place in This World." I sang it during one of the church services in front of McMurdo Station's Admiral, Naval personnel, scientists, and civilians, receiving a letter of appreciation from both the Admiral of the base and the Commander of my squadron. It lifted the spirits and promoted positive behavior in an environment of high-stress duty and responsibility. This song was also a declaration of my life.

In the military, I had finally found my place in this world. Fitting in with work, friends, and the way the military operated became second nature to me. I was no longer someone on the outside, but a person who excelled and set the bar.

Chapter 17:

TRAGIC LEGACY

VXE-6 had an internationally known reputation for effectively completing its extremely dangerous scientific missions. Aircraft and aircrew traversed the Antarctic continent with a near, if not one hundred percent, mission rating during any given Antarctic support deployment, breaking records along the way. Grueling twenty-four-hour maintenance and flight schedules were maintained in season and off, resulting in an outstanding performance of all equipment and personnel involved in the missions. For one hundred percent mission completions, we received letters of commendation due to unmatched flying and outstanding maintenance department performance in support of Antarctic research, development, and support.

Pilots, copilots, and flight engineers flew the seven UH-1N helicopters and six LC-130 Hercules cargo planes with surgical accuracy despite unforgiving weather, unforeseen mechanical failures, and potentially fatal outcomes. The constant work the aircrew performed while flying all over the treacherous Antarctic continent inevitably resulted in tremendous wear and tear on every part of the aircraft, including the mechanics, hydraulics, airframe, paint, wheels, tires, and other systems and components, requiring periodical restoration at the highest level of maintenance, Depot level.

The Hercules XD-03 came due for its Depot Level Maintenance, or "D" level, and needed to be flown to Christchurch, New Zealand, for a fourth-eight-month overhaul, corrosion treatment, and systems update. This included the rebuilding and manufacture of subassemblies, airframe assemblies, and the manufacture of parts, modification, testing, reclamation, and recycling of any and all parts associated with XD-03. Over the last few years, the aircraft had ongoing oil leak issues and mechanical failures needing to be addressed, including a major strip-down and complete overhaul.

Each shop was notified that XD-03 was going to be flown to Christchurch for D level. Accordingly, every shop had one person in the squadron assigned to XD-03, ensuring expedient remedy of any problem should it arise during the flight. Within each of the squadron's maintenance shops existed an unspoken lottery system when it came time to choose who would travel with the plane. PR1 notified me that it was my turn to represent our aircrew gear shop, observing and addressing any issues concerning the aircraft's safety and survival equipment throughout the journey.

Being that I was one of the newer members of the squadron, especially within the aircrew survival equipment shop, PR1 asked me if I wanted to go based on the lottery draw. I immediately accepted the flight assignment. I felt confident and mentally equipped to take on the task at hand.

In a few days, the aircraft was loaded up with an extra engine and all the wiring. Mechanical, electrical, and hydraulic components were also loaded onto the plane, chained up, and strapped down by the loadmasters to prevent sliding of gear and possible injury to passengers. I put my flight suit on the same day the aircraft was loaded, and zipped it up.

Folding my dog tags inside my t-shirt, I put on my spit-shined black flight boots and SV-2B survival vest. It was equipped with everything necessary to help stay alive, should something go wrong on the trip, and had to ditch on land or in the ocean. I was ready, at least until some freak accident where I could freeze, be killed in a crash, or be eaten by sharks. These were just a few realities we trained to accept should it happen, and part of daily flying. NB-8 parachutes were also provided for the pilots and a few extra ones for passengers.

I hung out around a few maintenance shops talking to friends while other squadron personnel were still in full training and packing mode, waiting for the order to board. I was pumped to be leaving in August for Winter Detachment, or WinDet. This was a preparatory time, a month before the entire squadron took off for deployment. Aircraft and aircrew were set aside to arrive before anyone else to help unpack and set up shops and maintenance areas in Christchurch and Antarctica.

Since XD-03 needed to be gone over thoroughly, it would need to be sent in August to drop off some of the needed personnel for the startup of the spring scientific season, and then parked for "D," or Depot Level. Other crew and aircraft would go down in September, including our UH-1N helicopters that were packed two-deep inside our Hercules aircraft, blades folded back behind them like insects.

I stood around during the next hour mindlessly waiting, when the commanding officer of AntarcticDevronSix called out over the intercom for XD-03 pilots, crew, and shop personnel designated to go, to load up. Suddenly, anxiety mixed with excitement engulfed me, and I swallowed hard. Out of nowhere, I had a flood of memories of all of the tragic stories and ill-fated history of previous XD flights, but there was no time for these thoughts.

I shook off my fear, walked over to the port side of the aircraft, and climbed the crew steps. Walking into the cargo area, I was hit with familiar smells of fireproof covering, insulation, oil, aircraft fuel, and webbing fixtures. When the last of the personnel boarded the plane, we were instructed to strap down with the seatbelts on the webbed seating and prepare for takeoff. Staring out the port window at the giant turbojet engine, I suddenly realized that, for better or worse, I was now a part of this XD-03 crew.

The pilots slowly coasted onto the flight line with engines blasting, lined the nose up on the middle of the runway to take off, and waited to hear the go-ahead from the flight control tower. The four Pratt and Whitney engines whistled through their powerful turbo props, and the engines roared to life. One at a time, all four giant propellers gained speed and momentum, moving an incredible amount of wind. The sheer sound of air being whipped and thrown behind the aircraft is something I will never forget. The entire fuselage reverberated with a throbbing, mechanical heartbeat coming from all four Allison T56, 4,695-horsepower engines. The LC-130 was vastly overpowered when designed and built, which made it an amazingly well-suited aircraft for missions across the harshest and most unforgiving continent on Earth. I was snapped out of my zoned-out gaze of listening and feeling the engines when the aircraft started moving. It gathered speed very quickly and shot down the runway faster and faster, lifting its nose steeply at full throttle, gaining adequate altitude to clear the California Mountains in the near distance.

After the plane leveled off, we settled in for the twenty-one or so hours of flight to Christchurch. Back then, we did not have cell phones, iPads, or personal laptop computers, so some took a nap, played cards, ate from their box lunches, or read a book. For sleeping, there was a small cot on the port and starboard sides of the fuselage that was hung up high on racks and fastened with clips.

Accessing the cots was by climbing a ladder leading up and above the strapped-down cargo. Passengers in the cargo took turns taking a quick nap on them. Otherwise, we slept wherever we could, including the webbed seats, floor, and on top of pallets strapped down with cargo.

In the cockpit, pilots and co-pilots had a bench area to rest, read, or take a nap. There was also a cubby hole above the bench seat behind the flight navigator's station. It was small, but flying twelve hours straight, as our pilots often did, made the turnaround from Christchurch with a change-out crew to pick up scientists and back to Antarctica, a bit less arduous.

The rudimentary toilet facilities in the back of the plane included a bucket with removable plastic liners below a toilet-like seat lid until it could be removed from the aircraft. It included a small curtain for privacy, if you could call it that. The top of the bathroom was completely open, so everyone and their grandma could hear and smell what was going on inside. Needless to say, I rarely ate before a flight, and rarely during one.

I was hanging out, taking a few pictures of the interior and the sky through the portholes. Then I heard someone say it was my turn to sleep on the cot if I wanted the spot. Man, those words were music to my ears. I tried sleeping on the angled-up cargo ramp, making up the rear panel of the aircraft. I could have stretched out on it if not for the floor rollers set in racks and the reverberating noise from the engines shaking my bones through the metal and aluminum LC-130 airframe skeleton. Oh yeah, and the fact that the ramp was only a few feet thick from death was pretty freaky, too.

I climbed up and laid down on the much needed smaller than a twin bed cot on the upper left of the airplane. All around me was cargo strapped and covered with cargo nets, but I could not have cared less. In the military, you slept whenever and wherever you had the chance. I fell fast asleep to the engine noise creeping its way past my ear protection, which by now was welcomed white noise. I did not know how long I was out when the loadmaster shoved me, saying to quickly climb down and head to the back of the plane near the ramp.

Without even thinking, I instinctively climbed down from the cot, saw that everyone who was once sitting was now standing closely together, looking towards the front of the aircraft. I immediately turned and noticed a thick, grayish-blue smoke starting to slowly fill up the entire cargo bay, creeping into the cockpit. Being in survival gear mode, I quickly realized that if the smoke's source could not be discovered and vented out of the aircraft, we were going to die from asphyxiation. This probability would only add to the aircraft's already tragic legacy, having more than its share of incidents starting decades earlier.

In the early part of 1960, JD-0321, as XD-03 was known at the time, was the first of several LC-130 aircraft outfitted for the Antarctic Development Squadron base in Point Mugu, California. The multi-million dollar front and rear skis, and every conceivable piece of state-of-the-art scientific support and research gear of its time, deemed it to be a very solid, dependable, and durable workhorse for all types of Antarctic missions.

In late 1971, after making several trips to the South Pole, JD-321 picked up a few French scientists who were working on a glaciology project and headed for the Russian Antarctic base Vostok. Seconds after takeoff, less than a hundred feet off the ground, one of the Jet Assisted

TakeOff (JATO) rockets attached to the port (left) side of the plane dislodged, shooting through the rear left tailpipe of the inboard left engine, blowing it up. The shattered fragments of the propeller knocked off the number one port engine, and its propeller flew off, burying twenty feet into solid ice. The nose ski mounts were shoved through the floor of the cockpit between the pilot and co-pilot, and propeller fragments sliced into the fuselage, destroying the inside of the cargo area. Miraculously, it landed with no deaths, but the aircraft was torn up beyond flight readiness.

Over the next three days, the crew battled snowstorms and extreme Antarctic temperatures well below negative 50 degrees Fahrenheit. With a temporarily built shelter made from the fuselage of the aircraft and onboard survival food, clothing, and gear, they had no choice but to wait until a rescue party was finally able to find and rescue them. Over the next seventeen years, the heavily damaged aircraft was completely covered by snow and ice, with only two feet of exposed tail. Attempting to dig out the plane twice during this time resulted in two deaths from two additional aircraft crashes. One plane was completely engulfed in flames, being totally destroyed near the initial crash site.

In the late 1980s, through a process that took about a month, the aircraft was dug out from its icy grave. All pertinent aviation systems were either replaced or repaired, and the plane was refitted with flight equipment successfully brought by another aircraft. It was raised from the dead, flown to Christchurch, updated and modernized, then renamed XD-03.

The loadmaster on our flight spoke through his headphones back and forth with the flight engineers and co-pilots. They began to systematically check every part of the aircraft that could contribute to the smoke now filling up the entire cargo area, becoming thicker and denser with each passing minute. The loadmaster quickly walked over to the starboard side and looked up into the right corner where bleed air came into the cargo bay, seeing that it was spewing thick, acrid smoke.

Come to find out, there was a massive fluid leak. All of the engines had stainless steel ductwork with various valves helping to control the output of the bleed air, regulate cabin pressure, and interior temperature via external vents that mixed outside air from the engines. One of the starboard engines had a bad valve, allowing air mixed with the smoke from heated, leaking fluid to go through the ductwork into the cargo area.

After addressing the problem and shutting down the engine responsible for compromising the bleed air system, specific valves were closed off. The poisonous exhaust and fumes were vented out of the cargo area, clearing up the pressurized interior of the aircraft. Within a few moments, everything was fine, except that we were now flying on three engines, not four. The aircraft could still fly pretty well on three turboprops, but our travel time to arrive in Hawaii for fuel would be delayed.

It was a miracle that nothing worse happened on the several-hour flight over nothing but water. More bleed air valves sticking, the bleed air system of the wing having multiple failures, or the engine catching fire due to excessive hot fluid leakage tripping an electrical fire, equated to a one-way ticket down to certain death. Landing in Hawaii, our mechanics on board assessed the damage to the aircraft.

Major repairs were mandatory, including replacement

of the engine and accompanying parts, and I did not have any problem whatsoever with that decision. I mean, c'mon, it was Hawaii, and we were living in the best hotel. Amazing food, able to proudly wear our Antarctic flight suits with an all-expenses-paid trip by Uncle Sam in paradise, and taking in the sights and sounds made this delay to New Zealand worth every second.

Our highly-trained mechanics were unbelievably skilled in knowing how to assess, identify, and fix any type of hydraulic, electronic, mechanical, or pneumatic issue with our aircraft. It took about two weeks total, waiting on the parts. Repairing the aircraft went pretty smoothly and faster than we thought. Our mechanics were some of the best technicians anywhere in the United States Navy, so fixing it adequately enough to fly XD-03 to our next stop, Pago Pago, American Samoa, was no problem.

Pago Pago is an extremely small island partially leased to America via an agreement by the reigning village chief. This agreement, in the late 1800s, between the United States and Pago Pago, later included takeoff and landing allowances on a 9,000-foot runway at Tafuna Airfield. This pit stop is used for refueling, rest, and minor maintenance of aircraft on the long journey between continents across the ocean. Many types of aircraft, including civilian cargo, private charter jets, Commercial airliners, and other military aircraft, also utilize the Island pit stop.

When we landed on the dark runway surrounded by the ocean, it had one hundred percent humidity, evident by thick sheets of moisture floating in the air. Immediately after unloading XD-03, my clothes were soaking wet. Needing to change, get some food, and rest, we checked into the administration office and received our room assignments. The next thing I knew, angry eyes from people who were very tall were staring us down.

The going story was that because we were Americans who used their island for landing and take-offs of our "loud and polluting aircraft," the native Samoan inhabitants did not like us very much, especially the military. This was confirmed when we were given rooms in the very back of the completely empty hotel, and had to haul all of our gear there. It sucked, but it was what it was.

The next morning, we rose early and mechanically assessed the aircraft before boarding. A discussion ensued to address what could be done about further mechanical problems now appearing. Some recommended that we stay in American Samoa to fix the potentially risky issues popping up after it was parked overnight. Even after the extensive mechanical delay in Hawaii to get us here on the trip, the old bird was still showing us some grief. However, after weighing the pros and cons of staying, it was mutually agreed upon to leave what was broken, or what could possibly break on the plane alone, and head to Christchurch.

Close to completing our mission to the New Zealand Antarctic Research base in Christchurch, we loaded up and closed the aircraft doors. We flew the rest of the trip and landed with no more incidents. My humble respect and honor will forever go to those brave men and women who flew, worked on, and took care of XD-0321/XD-03 Hercules, and all of the rest of the aircraft in our outstanding squadron, no matter the years served. This enduring aircraft, and the many crews who flew her all over the most unforgiving place on earth, had fought and overcome, despite casualties and setbacks.

XD-03 was retired from service and placed at the Davis-Monthan Air Force Base in Arizona after Antarctic Development Squadron Six was decommissioned in 1999. How the aircraft was finally laid to rest still seems unfitting for its astounding work history, its amazing crews that served aboard the aircraft, and the incredible missions accomplished. With everything that unbelievable workhorse endured and experienced, a place of honor in a museum would have been a much better end to this incredible machine.

A tribute to all of the men and women who flew, worked on, and loaded and unloaded this incredible aircraft on a wall somewhere in a museum would have also been a good start. Unfortunately, this was the proverbial end to the bittersweet story of a plane that will forever live in my heart and mind. I will never forget the adventure, shock, relief, and personal growth I experienced, being a proud part of the XD-03 legacy.

Dr. Eric Shannon Parr

Chapter 18:

INVENTION

As an aircrew survival equipment expert, I was specifically trained in inspecting, repairing, and maintaining extreme cold weather prototype and traditional survival gear of aircraft and aircrew, for any type of environment presented. I could pack any kind of personnel or cargo parachute. Wing-installed life rafts with survival packs were second nature and felt like I could pack them in my sleep.

I was also trained in on-board liquid oxygen systems, hearing protection, aircraft helmets, and audio equipment. Across the street from the squadron in Pt. Mugu, California, at "I" or Intermediate level maintenance, I was instructed in how to work on floatation devices, explosive-initiated seating for fighter jets, yet more styles of personal parachutes, and many other types of survival equipment. Additionally, I performed extensive organizational and intermediate levels of repair and preparation, including reconditioning and inspections.

School gave me an exhaustive knowledge base of gear. This helped to keep the mission on time and effective, and aircraft and aircrew were protected and functioning perfectly in real time. Training beyond school catapulted my knowledge base beyond what I ever expected, and it continued throughout my Naval service.

I learned how to create survival bags, initiate and sew up SV-2B survival vests and flight suits, and create seating covers for our aircraft. I also developed innovative ways to keep our UH-1N helicopters from flipping upside down in the 100-mile-an-hour-plus snowstorms. I was hanging out in the shop after completing inspections of several life vests when PR1 told me there was a call that came into the shop, specifically for me.

Surprised, I picked up the phone and answered it. On the other end was the Commanding Officer of my squadron. He asked if I could create something for our helicopters to keep them from flipping over when Herbie storms came around. Humbled, I said "Yes, Sir!" to the task of designing a piece of equipment to keep our helicopters stable in dangerous, environmental landing zones.

After accepting the challenge, I looked around the shop to see if there was any equipment I could modify or get ideas from to start the building process. I soon realized that after going through the PR shop, some kind of device had to be created from scratch. I walked outside and down the icy road to the helicopter hangar.

Going to the nearest helicopter parked in the landing zone, I stood there wondering what the heck I was going to do to keep it from flipping in bad weather. Then, out of nowhere, God began downloading ideas and thoughts. Since wind catches the UH-1N blades when it takes off in flight to get it airborne, creating something to keep the blades down and preventing wind from lifting the helicopter off the flight pad could be the solution.

Then this picture appeared in my mind. I envisioned a sock-like attachment that fit onto the blades, keeping the bird from moving in high winds. After a few measurements, I had what I needed.

I hurried back to my shop and began working on some designs, drawing up a sort of sock-like boot. I found some one-inch parachute webbing and canvas material, and started sewing some prototype models. For the next several hours, I tried different methods of sewing, combined with various shapes and sizes of material.

For the next two work shifts, I tried to make different types of blade holders. I took the canvas and sewed it up by itself, but being that it was not stiff and strong enough, this prototype was sure to rip because of the sharp helicopter blades. The webbing on its own would be durable enough, but would take much longer to complete, inevitably being too costly and inefficient. I ended up solving the problem by using both the canvas and the webbing in my design.

For my "Helo Blade Boot," I pre-measured and cut

out the white canvas and the blue one-inch wide webbing according to my measurements of the blades. Then, working from the inside out, I sewed the canvas together, and using box and repeated stitching, sewed on the webbing and steel grommet holes to pull the cord through, allowing the cinching down of the blades. For my work in inventing this novel piece of equipment, my shop received a letter of commendation from the squadron commander. Because I refused to accept defeat in the midst of a challenge, I was rewarded, and my shop was highly esteemed from the top down.

Chapter 19:

JONAH EXPERIENCE

After serving honorably in the Navy and being promoted to Petty Officer Third Class, the time for me to depart military life was vastly approaching. I was now serving on my last deployment in Christchurch. It was a bittersweet, short stay of three and a half months. With all of the excitement of leaving, work was no longer a mental constant, although military bearing was a given.

I had saved up sixty days of leave and would be released from active duty into reserve status two months early in December 1995. I sensed PR1 and colleagues knew I had pretty much switched off my military discipline concerning work, and honestly, I did not care. I would miss close friends and experiences gained, and the Navy was good to me. But I had this sort of task-driven attitude when something was about to be completed, I reset my brain to take on the next endeavor. In the military, we called it Short-timer's syndrome.

Before I knew it, my time had arrived to deploy back to Point Mugu base. I cleaned out my barracks room, turned in my extreme cold weather survival gear, had my Christchurch base departure checklist signed off, and packed all of my belongings in my military duffel bag. After saying my goodbyes, I loaded up into the LC-130 and took off for California.

Back in Point Mugu, things were really quiet in the squadron. The aircraft hangar was shut down for overseas maneuvers, all gear was in storage, and all of the personnel had deployed. There were only a few of us still at the squadron, and they were actually NAWS military assigned to keep watch for us while we were away on maneuvers.

I was assigned to stand duty in the duty office stationed upstairs overlooking the hangar. My job was to inspect and look over the aircraft and overall building structures at NAWS. That was pretty cool.

It was at night, and I rode a tricycle around the base making sure the F-14 Tomcats, A-7s, F-18s, F-4s, and all the other aircraft and associated weapon systems were tucked away and safe in their hangars or securely parked on the ramp of the flight line. The beachfront was not very far away either, so I had to make sure no one was going to try to ambush the base via waterways. During the day, I had extra time to get my checkout list completed, tying up loose ends before I left the military.

I sold my Ford pickup truck the year before and made some money, so I also needed to look for another truck to drive home. Having saved up several thousand dollars, it was time to find another vehicle. I needed something that could carry my tools, a duffel bag of uniforms, and personal belongings. After looking around for a few weeks, I found my truck.

I purchased a 1974 Dodge three-quarter-ton pickup crew cab for a thousand dollars. Now, when I say that this truck was big, this is a huge understatement. The beast was faded Dodge blue with primed rear body panels by yours truly, and four full doors. It had all the character and drivability of a boat, and it was love at first sight.

Inside the truck, two bench seats could fit six people easily. I bought aggressive tires that hummed on the road, and the sucker was so heavy it did not move when I jumped on the chrome rear bumper. It was twenty-two feet in length with a dry weight of fifty-eight hundred pounds before I put fuel into the two gas tanks. The engine was massive and got about nine miles a gallon on a good day. It was awesome.

We had a do-it-yourself maintenance shop on base with every conceivable tool. There was a car lift to get under the vehicle to change oil, repair mufflers, check your transmission, and anything else your vehicle needed. This was heaven to me. I repaired the small rusted-out holes in the floorboard on the passenger side, removed the trim on the truck body, put a new intake manifold on the engine with a carburetor, and tried to make sure everything was a go for the long trip home to Louisiana. Next was my last military physical, or exit exam. The female doctor had me lie face-up on the table, and looking me up and down, she said, "Well, you're a fine specimen, aren't you?" I just laughed out loud and said, "Yes, Ma'am."

I was in pretty good shape. I knew it. But the way she said it, while looking at me, actually made me feel a little embarrassed. Any other time, I would have responded a different way. Maybe I was just focused on leaving the military, and nothing else mattered at that moment, not even a forward, flirty comment from a hot female commissioned officer.

The Lieutenant asked me if I had anything physically wrong or any concerns she needed to know about. I shook my head and told her Nope. That was it.

No examination, no prodding, and no X-rays. I was done in five minutes flat. That was the fastest process for anything I had experienced concerning the military in four years.

The next day, I turned in my base check-out list at the personnel processing office, jumped into my truck, and rolled out. I could not believe it. After everything I had experienced, seen, and overcome, this chapter of my life had quickly ended.

My mind reeled with everything I had learned. The missions I survived. The places I had seen.

Friends I made, and the personal, spiritual, and professional changes I experienced, swirled through my brain. There was so much to think about. I saluted the gate guards, turned right onto the highway, and with eyes straight forward, I looked onto my next adventures. What would happen next?

Four years in the United States Navy went fast. I mean, when I was in the middle of whatever I was facing or doing, it was slow in its own right. But comprehensively, I cannot remember a single idle moment. There were crappy times, but looking back on them, they melded into the positive, giving me feelings to relish, reinforcing a deep respect for the military and the courage, sacrifice, and devotion given to it.

These years of serving with excellence, honor, and commendation in the United States Navy performing my job, adapting to changes, and overcoming impossibilities were priceless to me, chock full of lessons learned. Preparing for deployment and flights to Point Mugu, the endless survival gear equipment inspections, physical fitness tests, performance evaluations, and proficiency testing were all behind me. Near-death experiences and helping others pass through them solidified an enduring Antarctic research, development, and support legacy of Antarctic Development Squadron Six, of which I will always be a part. Go Navy.

It was a beautiful day for traveling in California, as it usually was. In December, it was about 65 degrees Fahrenheit, sunny, and a little windy. The weather is something I always miss. Oh, and heading out to the beaches after work. I was a little spoiled for sure during the off months, training for deployments.

Drinking my coffee in the truck cab, I carefully highlighted the route on my map across Interstate I-10, the southernmost main route across the bottom of the United States. It extended from San Diego, California, to Jacksonville, Florida, and seemed to be the best and safest way to travel. My route extended down South, going from California, through Arizona, New Mexico, Texas, then Louisiana, where mom and dad lived.

With the mechanical work I had done on the truck, it was working pretty well. The engine seemed strong and kept going. The heater and air conditioner did not work, but I couldn't have cared less. The radio was busted, so I used my portable compact disc player with old computer speakers on the dashboard.

I had to stop more often than not to refill the standard and reserve gas tanks because the gas gauge stopped working right before I started on my trip. No biggie, I thought, I will just stop every couple of hundred miles and top it off. I guessed nine miles per gallon before starting the trip, but I really did not know how much the truck could get, so I anticipated not wanting to get stuck in the middle of the Arizona desert or Texas Plains. Constantly addressing the fuel issue put me at peace, saying out loud that this trip was going to be a breeze. I should not have made this prediction.

Within the first five hundred miles, things started to go haywire. I was driving down I-10, and out of nowhere, my truck started to sputter and jerk, making weird noises. My speed was never constant, and I lost a lot of power, slowing down enough to count the white lines separating the left from the right traffic lanes. I guessed about thirty-five or forty miles an hour was the pace I was now keeping in the Dodge.

So there I was, driving down the road slow as a snail, and there was nothing to be done but make sure I was still driving forward, no matter the speed. During the day, cars would fly by and trucks with no doors that looked like they should not have even been able to run would smoke, sputter, and wobble past me. It was a shameful, frustrating, and pride-swallowing time. My ego was bruised, and as the trip progressed, I began to feel fearful, angry, and helpless. At night, especially in Arizona, it was freezing. The desert was hot during the day, but at night the temperature dropped significantly. Because my truck had bad door seals, it allowed freezing air in. The temperature inside the cab of the truck dropped drastically, and there was nothing I could do to stop it.

In Antarctica, I became somewhat accustomed to being exposed to extreme cold weather. It was funny how situations, purpose, and training shifted my perspective. Staying and managing extreme cold was a mandatory part of serving in the United States Navy, but I was no longer part of the true snowy South. Now was the time to get home. I think that not having control over my environment in some way added to my frustration and amplified the effects of the cold.

To keep from feeling like I was freezing to death, I had to tuck myself down between the front door edge and the dash, holding the steering wheel with both hands, with my chest on the left-hand edge of the wheel. To see where I was on the road, I looked out the front windshield to the left corner of the hood of the truck, trying to keep it lined up with the middle intermittent white lines. The wind bleeding through the edges of the door created a constant loud air pressure noise like a tire having its air let out through the bleed valve, amplified a hundred times over.

Going back to how fast I could go on the trip, my truck had lost a lot of power by the following day. The engine itself was good, but the exhaust manifold seals were bad. For those mechanics out there, and maybe those who are not, there are a couple of metal objects called exhaust manifolds. These are attached to the engine on both sides that connect to the headers, then the tailpipe that extends out the back of a vehicle, taking the exhaust from the motor out the rear of a vehicle.

About halfway through the trip, the old exhaust manifold seals blew out, causing a reduction in back pressure from the motor, resulting in loss of power. This loss yielded decreased capability of the truck to climb hills, stay at constant speeds, and have any kind of reliability.

Slow speeds meant staying on the road longer, stretching out the trip over several days. I refused to accept the delay in travel time, so I stopped and bought some anti-sleeping pills, coffee, and stomach medicine. I was set on not letting this trip defeat me.

Deciding from the beginning of my trip to get home in a reasonable amount of time, I stopped only to get gas and over-the-counter drugs to stay awake. I even refused to eat except for one time in Texas at a steakhouse, because I thought it would slow me down. And this is when I drank coffee, I took stomach meds to coat it, trying to keep my digestive track from being engulfed in acid.

One of the many times I stopped for fuel, day and night, the truck refused to start. It took several attempts to turn the key until it roared to life. God gave me a creative miracle, albeit a mechanical one. Now I had to keep the truck running at gas stations and not pull off the road at rest stops, because getting stranded in the middle of nowhere was not my first choice.

I did stay at a hotel only once because I was becoming delirious a few days into the trip after no sleep and constant driving. Thankfully, the truck did start because I forgot in my extreme fatigue that I could not let the engine die. Admittedly, I was too hardheaded to think of any other way to make the trip easier than not to eat or sleep, driving twenty-four hours a day until I arrived home in Louisiana.

Pissed off and determined not to be deterred from my goal, I pushed through it all. Something else occurred during my fits of anger. I started to cry out to God. It was as if my very soul was being emptied out, praying for Him to get me home.

I knew God had intervened in my life and helped me in difficult circumstances in the military, yet the deep relationship I used to have with Jesus Christ was forgotten through my own selfishness. I refused to talk to God unless I needed help out of difficult circumstances. I had been living for me and what I wanted to do, not for Him.

I was driving at night through Texas when out of nowhere, I saw this flash of brown shoot across the road. A deer ran straight for me and smashed into my front bumper, but rolled off as I continued driving. A few minutes later, another one did the same thing, but hit the front of my truck in such a manner that it caused my hood to shoot up.

Upon the second impact of the deer, the hood unhinged, shot straight up, and wrapped itself over the front windshield. I slowly drove two miles on the side of the road with my head sticking out the window to the next gas station. I was beyond mad, shocked, and pretty out of it, so stopping to stretch was a good idea anyway.

I took my tools out and took off the hood. Then, out of nowhere, I suddenly lost it. I threw the hood down on the ground, jumped on top of it, and started laughing and crying at the same time at the top of my lungs. It was as if I just broke apart emotionally, and I refused to give a crap one way or the other who saw.

All of my stress, fear, anxiety, and ego just bubbled up at the same time, exploding into a loud exclamation of spiritual release. People all around just stared at me. I felt that my entire being was coming unhinged, saying to the hood and my circumstances, "Hallelujah! Thank you, Jesus! You will not defeat me, devil!"

I threw that old, bent-up hood into the back of my truck, put it in drive, and drove out of the gas station. From that moment on, I was set free from my fear and anxiety, beginning the process of allowing God to clean out the bad and fill me up with His peace and redemptive happiness. But he was not finished with me on the trip.

A couple of hundred miles from Baton Rouge, the fan that turns to keep the engine cool exploded and ripped through the radiator, causing coolant to go everywhere. Now, I had to stop every few miles to put water in the radiator. If I had not, the engine might have overheated to the point of blowing up.

Words cannot express how relieved I was at making it to my parents' house. I hugged my mom as if I had not seen her forever. Truth be told, I really only saw them three times in four years. Refusing to go home was a choice not based on duty requirements, but solely on having to deal with dad's relentless, controlling attitude.

I slept for two days straight, only getting up to use the bathroom. I had no idea how worn out I was from that trip. It took a mental and physical toll on me, still feeling the road vibrations of the truck while sleeping, days after the trip ended.

It was like an extreme case of jet lag, but from driving so long and so far. My whole body felt like a lead weight, and walking was really hard to do. My mind was in a haze, and I dismissed everything and everyone for hours on end until I could get rested up.

God used this trip to jar loose dependence on myself and reset my focus on God, triggering a repentant heart. I asked forgiveness for everything I had done that displeased the Lord. At night, I would get so cold, so lonely and afraid, thinking my truck would stall out in the middle of the dark desert or on the highways that I cried out, repenting for all of the misdeeds, rebellion, and disobedience. I vowed to serve God and get myself right in his eyes. I did this continuously at night during the trip until I felt clean, full of peace, knowing that my life was resetting for the better.

In the Navy, I learned how to rely on my shipmates, but failed to keep God in the picture. He did speak to me in circumstances, thoughts, and deep feelings, but I still did my own thing despite supernatural intervention in the midst of chaos. When God had me all alone in the middle of that freezing desert on a lonely road, and away from anything or anyone that could help, I was left with nothing but Him. This turned out to be my Jonah experience.

In the Bible, Jonah refused to obey the Lord, as I had done in the Navy. I partied, slept with women, and did my own thing. When Jonah was told by God to go preach to Nineveh, he refused and did his own thing, eventually being thrown overboard, where a whale swallowed him up for three days and nights. God had Jonah in a place where all he could do was cry out and pray that God would redeem his situation and save him.

Similarly, I escaped into my own world, doing my own things, refusing to hear and obey God's voice. On this trip, God used situations out of my control to get my attention and held me captive for three days and nights, where it was just me and Him. I was in the belly of my own personal whale, as it were. I had to have total reliance on God to save me through everything I was experiencing, or let me die. And I'm so very glad he brought me through it all.

Chapter 20:

BUILDING A BUSINESS

Over the next year and a half, I decompressed from serving in the Navy. Staying busy, I helped mom and dad fix their house, rebuilt the motor in my Dodge, and looked for work. I even took the empty back third of the house and remodeled it into an apartment.

Instead of paying rent to dad, I fixed up that space into a pretty slick bachelor pad, complete with bathroom, living room, kitchen, bedroom, and installed working appliances. It was a cool way to get reaccustomed to civilian life. And of course, there were no free lunches, especially for someone's son who just returned from the United States Navy; sarcasm inferred.

Conforming to real life without some sort of veteran transition therapy or talking to other vets who had separated from the Navy was pretty crazy. It felt like I was now in a false reality, whereas before the military had been the real thing. To help my mind adjust as a civilian, painting became my therapeutic tool.

Additionally, I started going to a local church and got plugged into the choir and music ministry there. I felt closer to God and wanted to serve Him with my gifts, so I auditioned and got a role in the massive choir ensemble that sang in the main services on Sunday. It was a real blessing, and I thoroughly enjoyed the interaction with others who shared similar interests. I also rededicated my life to God, having professed the sin in my life and not living the way I should have while in the military.

I continued to practice and perfect my painting and staining craft on the rest of Dad's house over the next year and a half. Granted, the remodeled garage was not the ideal color design, but it gave me the opportunity to try different methods of taping, staining, and custom color matching. I became so proficient at what needed to be done in terms of the paint trade that I started a residential and commercial painting contracting business after moving to Nashville, Tennessee.

I had lived there on and off from the time I was a teenager until I left for the military. I was pretty familiar with how things worked and had some friends to reconnect with. It was a pretty easy move, and exponentially better than the ridiculously crazy trip from California to Louisiana.

I heard of a woman who sometimes rented out her basement to people who had proven to be good tenants. Since my brother knew her, I came with a great reference.

From there, I launched my high-end home improvement company, specializing in custom color matching, staining, remodeling, and building furniture. I also catered to interior aesthetic designs. Dad was an entrepreneur, and my grandfather before him was one, as well, and an inventor, so it ran in the family. I did not have any formal training in how to start a business. I had seen how dad ran his business, but never learned the practical steps of a business model. I only observed what was done to start and operate one, as well as what not to do when operating a company.

What I did have was grace, knowledge, and favor from God. I was very resourceful and observant, and having creativity helped me to develop my painting craft. I also discovered an exclusively wealthy neighborhood in Nashville. Seeing that several houses looked like they needed the exteriors painted, I slipped a flier into the door handle of a random three-story house. I told the owners who I was, what I offered, and I prayed I would get a response.

The next day, I received a call from the owner, who also happened to be the founder of a large dry-cleaning business in town. He wanted me to paint the outside of his house and write down the amount it would cost on a piece of paper. I pitched him an amount of forty-seven hundred dollars, and he took the bait. I could not believe it. God blessed me beyond measure.

This was my very first job as a painting contractor, and the entire exterior only took a few weeks to complete. He liked what I did and wanted the interior painted as well. That cost him sixty-eight hundred dollars. And God blessed me, yet again. From then on, I would get large residential properties to paint, mostly with just the mention of my name. My reputation grew for being good at what I did, so much so that in a few months, I stopped having to advertise.

People knew I was the only contractor to get their work done right the first time, and I only worked on one job at a time, ensuring it was perfect. I also suggested specific colors with various types of furniture that the clients held in each room. Interior decorators complimented me on my skills, noticing I had an eye for interior aesthetics and how it affected the client's specific settings in various types of living areas. I was asked if I might ever start an interior decorating business. Complimentary as it was, I did not see this as part of my future.

In the few years following, I gradually became more and more deprogrammed from all of the Navy-instilled behavioral and psychological mindset. I held on to great memories of the United States Navy, friendships I developed, and incredible experiences I will never forget. The discipline, focus, attention to detail, and persistence to complete any task presented to me that began to develop in my younger years were cemented in my character during my service. In 2001, I made the jump to continue my education, and I am glad I did, because the country as a whole would forever be changed.

Chapter 21:

OLD COLLEGE TRY; AGAIN

I would be remiss if I did not mention this moment in American history, both as a significant shifting moment in my life and one that shook the very foundations of our great nation. This is not a political statement or a way to invoke debate between me as a writer and those who may not agree with my views about September 11, 2001. It is simply a time in my life that impacted me, as it did many others, sobering all of us to new realizations because this horrible incident happened. We all had to readjust our priorities, perceptions, and convictions to what it meant to be a citizen of this great nation, the United States of America.

I was in the paint shop when the Twin Towers were hit, and I will never forget how I felt seeing my country attacked by an enemy hell-bent on destroying everything I stood for, both as a United States Naval veteran and a patriot. Many men and women who have served or are still serving in the military, much better than I will ever hope to be, have sacrificed their lives defending the greatest nation on the face of the earth. My heart and salute go out to them and their families, and I will forever be in their debt.

I was dumbfounded as to the extent and breadth of the enemy's attacks, and equally so from the look on the painter's reactions in the shop. From a store that was usually busting with laughter, stories about customers, and asking about orders being picked up, to no sound at all, it was like people were afraid to even move. You could hear an ant's pin drop.

We just stared at the small television on top of the counter and knew everything would be different. I watched the horrific news for a while longer, paid for my supplies, and walked out of the store shaking my head. New York had its immediate concerns and dangers, affecting every area of the country. Where I lived, we were very shaken up, but I had to keep a professional and personal perspective as well.

In the same year of this horrific event, I returned to school and went after my education with dedicated fervor and renewed appreciation of what education meant to me. I became acutely aware of how it could afford opportunities for a career and made sure I did not take it for granted. I had achieved top academic levels in the military, individually and as a class, during training. It helped me to develop self-respect and concrete mental potential to excel beyond my previous academic suppositions. It was now time to do it in the real world, going all in, building on success already established.

I attended a small community college down the road

from my house called Volunteer State Community College, and learned that my grades were better the second time around, but not great on account of not being a very good student. The weird thing was that I excelled academically in the military under extreme, stressful conditions, but not in a normal environment. Was it because I had been trained to work better under pressure? Could my new way of attacking academics be hinged on allowing me to get into tough positions, so that the only way to get out of them was to create stress as fuel to succeed?

In addition to work and academics, I got involved in the college theater company and acted in different types of plays, from musicals to dramas. Still dealing with rejection issues popping up now and then, making myself get out there and develop friendships with teachers, professors, and fellow students was healthy and a good addition to my life. Being elected Vice-President of the theater club, Delta Psi Omega, for a year rewarded my actions of reaching out and made me feel accepted as a leader in the theater community. I found interacting with others to be a pleasure and not an annoyance, engaging with people freely without pushing them away.

One of my favorite classes in community college was psychology. I learned how people acted and reacted based on mental, emotional, internal, and external stimuli. I also learned that certain causes trigger certain people to act one way in an environment, while others display other types of behavior.

This subject opened my eyes to the effects and results of interior and exterior factors of an individual placed inside and outside of any particular type of environment, at various stages in life. I gained top scores in this class, setting me on a path to pursue similar academic interests later. It also foreshadowed my future endeavors, giving me an intimate glimpse into my personal, psychologically-based actions and reactions.

After graduating in 2003 with an associate's degree in University Studies with average scores, I started my bachelor's that fall in Psychology at Middle Tennessee State University. While pursuing my bachelor's, I realized a love for the deviant psychology curriculum and the many different layers of behavior and emotional levels in the field.

During our studies, we delved deep into the minds of those who had malevolent behaviors caused by either direct physical damage to the brain or indirect emotional or social harm, causing Post Traumatic Stress Disorder. Texts displayed many unique and unbelievable situations of individuals who earned a place in the history books. One such person was Phineas Gage, a railroad worker from the 1800s. He drilled and laid the charges composed of gunpowder in the holes for the spikes. Being a mild-mannered man, everyone liked him and considered Phineas to be a great team leader and railroad worker.

One afternoon in 1848, Phineas was tamping the gunpowder in the rocky ground with a long, steel rod when a spark caused the charge to go off, shooting the steel rod from his hand at an angle below the left cheekbone, through the lower part of the skull, exiting out the left frontal lobe. The nearby doctor ran over, assuming he was killed. Still breathing, he was rushed to the doctor's office.

The surgeon inspected the hole, realizing the extensive damage showed a mostly destroyed left side of the brain and a massive loss of tissue. The exam included putting his fingers through both the top and bottom of Phineas' skull, being able to touch them together. He cleaned out the dirt and rocks, then packed the hole with rags to stop the bleeding after removing any loose brain matter.

Instead of being killed, Phineas lived out the next several years, but now with radically changed behavior, including bouts of lashing out in anger at everyone. He also had sporadic fits of anxiety, fear, and acute swings of emotional outbursts. A man who should have certainly died went from a calm, engaging, and happy individual revered by all to a mentally unstable individual dying from wound-induced epileptic seizures twelve years later.

After class, I would be one of the first to ask questions, gleaning every piece of information from the lecture presented. She also gave us tidbits of information, like Phineas' skull being on display to this day at Harvard Medical School for study on how the brain responds and compensates to extreme trauma. A patient woman who was always open to chat, my professor's influence helped shape my love for Psychology. Every day was something new to realize as my Bachelor's pursuit continued, and some things I learned impacted me in ways I never saw coming.

Chapter 22:

KIDNEY PUNCTURE NEEDLES

I was headed to class on a windy morning when out of nowhere, something blew into my eye, and it hurt like anything. After a few minutes of trying to get whatever was in it out, I decided to miss class and headed straight to the campus clinic. After waiting several minutes, a nurse brought me back to a table and I lay down. She poked and prodded around my eyelids for only two minutes, then gave me a bill for sixty bucks.

This was ridiculous and expensive, especially for a poor student. I knew I had to get better medical care than that. Sitting in class, my eye was still hurting, and the eye cream did not do anything for me.

I had this sudden thought of being in the service, and remembered that in the Navy, I had free, full medical coverage, not having to worry about any health issues being covered even after my military career. Eyes, ears, nose, and throat, everything was covered. But even if I became sick in the Navy, I never told anyone, because we were supposed to be tougher than the flu, and we were trained to deal with it. I never missed a day of work in my entire time in the military, only taking a few hours off for a wisdom tooth extraction, returning to work that evening.

As a veteran who served honorably in the United States Navy for four years, I was very thankful to have full access to free healthcare and other medical services. After doing some research, I found out about the Nashville Veterans Affairs Medical Center adjacent to Vanderbilt University. I drove around downtown, trying to get myself reacquainted until locating the veteran's hospital.

Vanderbilt University Medical Center had physicians, doctors, surgeons, interns, fellows, and residents who worked at the veterans' hospital, and was known for its excellence in medical practice, teaching, and research. Considering Vanderbilt was one of the top Ivy League universities in the United States, I surmised the veteran's hospital had an excellent chance of being an outstanding medical facility.

After school, I drove over to enroll in the veteran hospital. The check-in with the receptionists who assisted me in getting plugged into the system went very smoothly. My name, address, social security number, form DD-214 showing date of discharge from the military, and a whole host of other veteran-specific information were taken and entered into the hospital database.

Nurses took my vitals and some blood and gave me a thorough checkup. I also completed a general health questionnaire and other requirements. After enrolling, the nurse told me I might receive a phone call if anything popped up, but not to worry because I presented as a very healthy individual. It felt great knowing my health needs would be in good hands, for free.

Two days later, I received a call, and a nurse on the other end of the line asked me a few questions covering mental assessments, how I was feeling, and others. Then, out of nowhere, she bluntly requested that I come in for a chat in a few days. I said I could be there tomorrow, she set the appointment verbally, and hung up.

I drove to the hospital that next afternoon, checked in, and waited. What were they going to tell me? Maybe they lost one of my medical files?

It did not take long before I was called back to a private room. I sat down, and the nurse sat down in front of a computer screen, asking me how I had been. After a few minutes of talking, she turned in her seat to explain what the computer monitor was displaying.

On it was a graph with words, numbers, and different colored lines going from down to the left, climbing up to the right. There was a green line and a red line, with the green line going straight across and the red line climbing beyond the green, to the top of the graph. Showing me this chart on the computer screen, the nurse explained that the green line represented a base level of normal creatinine, and the red indicated a climbing level.

Based on the representation of lines and numbers, my blood levels indicated a much higher than normal creatinine level of 0.9 to 1.0. In fact, mine had reached 4.7 with a noted pattern to rise. According to her, this indicated a highly negative result.

Even after explaining to me all of the signs, verbiage,

and medical concerns, I still had no idea what I was looking at or why it was so alarming. After a few minutes of talking to me, the concerned nurse said the hospital needed to do a test to determine the reason for the significant rise in creatinine.

She added that we should not jump ahead of these results either, because high muscle content when one is or was a bodybuilder can be a factor in the increase of creatinine. More lean muscle mass contributes to higher levels. It could also be a random spike in my levels for any number of reasons, so having a "minimally invasive" test using a needle inserted into my kidneys to take tissue samples could define the issue.

A few minutes later, a doctor came into the room to explain the kidney biopsy procedure. He would insert a long needle several times into both kidneys, making sure a comprehensive core sample of kidney tissue is obtained. At the time, it did not sound as horrific as it does now as I write these words. I told them I did not want to remember anything about that procedure, and they assured me this would be done.

Being held for observation after the procedure for a few days, nurses could measure the amount of blood in my urine until my urine showed no more traces of blood. After discussing the procedure in much detail, I was scheduled for the biopsy four days later. I left the hospital now concerned, but still not freaking out.

Over the next four days, I filled my time with work, school, and anything else that deterred me from thinking about that test. I stayed busy, immersing myself in things to avoid worrying about the inevitable. I controlled what I could mentally and vowed to let the rest take care of itself.

Sometimes staying busy was helpful, sometimes it was not. In this case, it worked like a charm. I worked out, painted a bit on a personal project, and mentioned nothing to anyone. Those who were closest to me, even family, knew nothing about the initial findings leading to the upcoming test. I did not want to upset anyone before I had learned of the results.

The day of the procedure, my mind was reeling. No matter how much pre-surgical information was given to me by the hospital staff, I really did not know what to expect. The whole kidney thing was all completely new to me. I mean, who thinks about internal organs as an athletic and very healthy twenty-something-year-old?

Four days later, I checked into the hospital and waited for my turn. No time went by until I heard the receptionist call out my name. Here we go. No turning back now.

As I walked up to an automatically opening door to the right of the gigantic waiting area, I was greeted by a smiling nurse who asked how I was doing. Considering I was about to have several holes punched into my kidneys with monster needles, I was surprisingly pretty okay. We walked down the corridor together, having some small talk, and turned down a hallway.

We walked through a taller-than-expected set of heavy, wooden double doors that closed automatically. We went down a long, flower wallpapered hallway and noticed it was getting progressively colder the further we walked. Turning a second corner, we entered a room filled with blood pressure and machines that took vitals.

The nurse gave me a thermometer and checked my temperature, then my blood pressure. She ran through a very thorough pre-surgical checklist specific to my case that took several minutes. It seemed as if an hour had gone by as the nurse asked me many questions, marking off her list as I answered.

"Fasted?" Check. "No water?" Check.

"Feel okay? Do you have someone who can stay with you after the procedure?" Check, check, and check.

Finally, after dozens of questions, I was escorted to my assigned hospital room, where I would stay before and after the procedure. I changed into a hospital gown, lay down, and tried to relax in the bed. Who was I kidding? There was nothing I could do to stay calm. I really needed that medication, which I was promised would help me calm down and forget.

A few nurses came into the room to prep me for the biopsy. One of them put an IV into the top of my hand, and the other asked me to put all of my clothes, my watch, and everything I owned into a personal locker with a key. A few minutes passed after I changed, and another nurse came into the room asking how I was doing, and a few more standard questions all hospital patients are asked.

As she turned around to leave, I asked about the miracle medicine I would be getting to help forget the procedure pain and process that was about to happen. Puzzled, the nurse asked me what I was talking about, and this really concerned me. I told her, again, that a pre-surgical medication was guaranteed to me by the doctor who would be conducting the procedure to relax my nerves and help me forget what was about to happen.

She reluctantly left the room with a serious, puzzled look on her face. After a few minutes, she returned with a tablet of medicine X. I took medicine X with water and waited for it to kick in. After fifteen minutes, I did not feel any different. I pushed the nurses' help button on the side of my bed, told them I was the kidney biopsy patient who had taken something to relax and help me forget things, and it was not working.

A couple more nurses came back into my room and were very concerned. I guess the staff thought that the medication given had a record of working on patients quickly, or I was lying about taking it. And it was a strong dose, but it had no effect, not even in the least.

So, the staff left my room and came back with medicine Y, then a few minutes later, medicine Z. The third one did the trick. Thirty minutes later, I was flying high, laughing, and completely out of it. I mean, I could not tell you my name if I tried. I was cautioned before being administered my meds to breathe when the doctors performing the procedure asked me to do so, but now I was only interested in how high I could climb the imaginary mountain outside my window.

A couple of porters who hauled around beds and patients all over the hospital appeared. They put me on a gurney, wheeled me down a freezing hallway, turned the corner, and entered a large operating room where I was met by my surgical team. Above a table was an oddly-shaped, rectangular-like machine reaching over with boxes, wires, and tubes coming out of the sides and the bottom of it. I assumed it was what they would be using to excavate my kidneys.

Being completely stoned from the medicinal concoction, I walked with assistance over to the table and lay face down on the cold procedure table. The doctors and nurses waiting inside the room positioned my body in such a way that my back was in direct line with what I nicknamed the "needle coring machine," and where my

IV would be readily accessible. The last thing I remember was a doctor yelling in my face to breathe.

Apparently, I had so much medicine that it caused me to not breathe in enough during the procedure to expand my diaphragm for the needles to core some of the samples. I was warned about this. The several-inch-long needle had to be strategically inserted into the exact, premeasured areas of the kidneys. Any deviation of the sharp instrument being inserted between organs, arteries, or blood vessels, internal bleeding, and death could be the inevitable outcome.

Thankfully, an adequate amount of tissue samples was withdrawn over the course of an hour, and the overall sampling was a great success. Still being completely out of it following the exam, I was wheeled back to my room. I did not remember a thing until my girlfriend at the time came into my hospital room and called out my name as I became coherent. With the surgery complete, all that was left was waiting for the results while my kidneys healed from several puncture wounds.

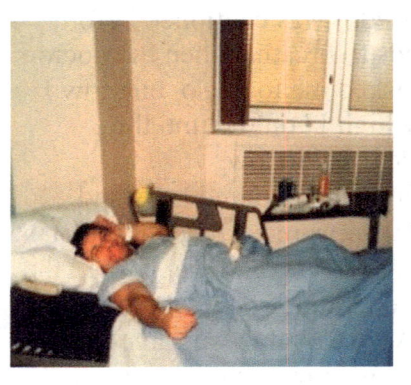

During the next three days of recuperation, doctors, nurses, and my surgeon came in and out, taking blood pressure, temperature, and several other vitals. Measuring how my kidneys were recovering was performed by urinating in collection containers every few hours. It turned out to be the best practical way to keep track of my health status post-procedure, putting the samples on the windowsill to observe.

Blood leaking from the puncture wounds in the kidneys collects in the bladder and is excreted from the body mixed with urine. By measuring the ratio of urine to blood in each bottle, the doctors saw how the puncture wounds in my kidneys were healing. I would be released from the hospital and able to go home when my urine output was clear and free from any significant signs of red blood cells.

I did not feel a thing until the pain meds wore off. The pain was almost unbearable in my back at first, but gradually became less and less as I healed. I had pain medication issued to me that did help a bit, helping me deal with sitting during college class lectures after a week of staying home. Gradually, over a period of several weeks, I felt strong enough to sit through a full lecture without a pillow against my back. Now, it was a matter of waiting for the phone call that would give me the results of the procedure.

A few weeks later, I was studying at home, pushing myself as a reformed procrastinator does, to finish past-due schoolwork due the next day. I heard the phone ring a few times, then walked over to the counter and picked up the receiver. Yep, it was a time when landlines were still in use.

A gentleman on the other end of the line introduced himself as Dr. James, Chief Nephrologist at the Vanderbilt University Medical Center. It was very important for me to come in and see him as soon as possible to let me know about the biopsy test results. I told him I would be there the next day. He seemed to be in a hurry and had to go, but said he would see me tomorrow at the agreed time.

We hung up, and my brain went a thousand miles an hour again. Was this going to be good news for me? Was this just the way they did things? Not being sick much at all, is this how it usually works with hospitals? Am I dying?

Nothing in detail was discussed concerning my health, and nothing more was said about my seemingly less-than-adequate test results. Man, let me tell you, I was concerned. An uneasy feeling crept up from deep inside my gut. Something was off about our conversation, but I could not put my finger on it.

The next day, while driving to the hospital, my uneasiness and flying negative assumptions were ever-present. After checking in, I sat down in the busy waiting area surrounded by veterans everywhere. I wondered how many of them were dying or there for just a routine checkup.

I saw this man in a wheelchair whose skin was green, and his eyes more yellow than mustard. I just stared at him, getting more and more nervous, until the nurse attending the information desk stood up. She leaned over towards me, called out my name, and snapped me out of it.

Walking down a long hallway, I turned to the left, walked around a row of chairs, and up between sickly people waiting for their turn. Heading down the main corridor, a doctor tilted his head out of a doorway, meeting my eyes with a look of seriousness. As I walked towards him, he asked how I was doing. I did not answer, but remembered that it was the same voice asking me to come back to the hospital to talk about my biopsy results. There was also another doctor in the room with him, who

I found out later was working on her fellowship in the Vanderbilt Hospital nephrology department.

He introduced himself again as Dr. James, Chief Nephrologist of the Vanderbilt University Medical Center. Asking me to sit down, he wondered if I had any pain. Not waiting for my reply, Dr. James said the results of my kidney biopsy, and asked if there was anyone waiting in the lobby because they should hear this news, too. I nervously said no, and then came the news that I was not really ready to hear.

There were definite indications of deterioration in the filtering systems in both of my kidneys. Excessive amounts of IgA, or Immunoglobulin A, existed in my kidneys, causing poisons and waste to not be excreted from my body due to faltering filtering systems. As a result, my kidneys had become severely damaged, starting the process of turning them into two clumps of non-filtering scar tissue.

Because of the scarring, my kidneys had reduced function, from a normal filtering of a hundred percent to only sixty-five percent between both of them. This combined number was left having to filter out all of the waste and toxins, balance body hormones, monitor glandular functions, and perform several other life-sustaining processes in my body.

Reduced function and other signs led to a diagnosis of IgA Nephropathy, a chronic disease that steadily reduces kidney function over a few or several years, depending on the level and type. This specific type of slowly progressing disease of the kidneys is nicknamed the "healthy man's disease." A person can have it for years or even decades without ever knowing it or having any indications until it has already done irreversible kidney damage. As was the case in my case, otherwise healthy individuals do not know they have it because they can go about life normally, working out and staying fit, until blood tests come back and reveal elevated creatinine levels.

According to the doctors, I could have had it since I was ten years old. I had a very slowly progressing type of the disease that could not be measured until enough scarring and damage occurred. To this day, doctors do not know what causes this disease, and there is no cure.

I just sat there stunned, speechless, and unable to comprehend what he said. He just stared at me with strict sincerity through the top of his glasses as the nephrologist fellow slowly walked over to my chair and tried to comfort me. She did not say a word as he proceeded to explain what would happen over the next few years.

My life span with the level of damage my kidneys had obtained was three to five years, best guess. During this time, my creatinine levels would continue to rise, indicating a gradual decline in kidney function. My filtering systems of the kidneys would become more and more scarred, causing a decrease in use and function.

Because of reduced cleaning of the blood through scarred filters caused by the inability of the kidneys to get rid of IgA, more and more poison from waste deposits, not being able to leave my body through excrement and urine, would stay in the blood. This meant, essentially, waste would increase slowly, poisoning my body until the kidneys shut down completely and I would die. Dr. James told me that the best way to get to the three to five-year mark of staying alive with the way my kidneys were presently functioning was to get into the best shape of my life.

I laughed out loud, almost hysterically. I was already in great shape, even with this diagnosis. I spent most of my life maintaining my health, not worshipping the sun, eating right, drinking lots of water, everything. What else could I do? I asked him what would happen to me at that point.

Dr. James looked right at me and said not to worry about the future. I turned and looked right into his eyes, and over to the fellowship doctor, telling them I believed in God. He would let me live as long as I needed to, because I was a believer. No matter what they or any other doctor in the hospital could tell me, God had all of this under control. And that was my resolve. Period.

Dr. James replied in an odd, surprising laugh, saying that it was good that I had this positive outlook. Looking at him, I could tell he was not in agreement with my prognosis of the kidney disease, but it did not matter. My God directed my life, not any person. Not even my body would stop when it wanted to, only when God wanted it to do so.

I slowly walked to my car, resolute in knowing God was in control, despite feelings of despair now slowly growing in the pit of my stomach. When I was about halfway to my apartment, a realization of everything said hit me right between the eyes, and I began denying everything that happened at the doctor's office. I had rededicated my life to God, knowing I was a follower of Jesus Christ, so why did I have to experience this horrible news? Does He not protect His people from sickness?

I rushed home and called my girlfriend, telling her everything that I was told. Then, I really lost it. I bent over, grabbed the back of my wooden desk chair, shook it and the phone, and screamed at the top of my lungs to

God, asking Him why I had to have this happen to me. I did not deserve this! I vented to her for over an hour and hung up. I knew from that moment that everything in my life would change.

So, there it was. I was diagnosed with an irreversible, incurable chronic kidney disease and had to face the irreconcilable fact that someday, however God chose, I would die or be healed in any way He saw fit. It took a few days to accept I was responsible to step out in faith and believe as I had professed to the doctors, no matter what. I had to choose to defy the lies of the doctors or live in a life of fear, anxiety, and desperation about this diagnosis.

It was time to get moving and grooving and not just sit around the apartment moping, waiting for the inevitable to happen. What kind of hypocrite would I be if I went back, regressed emotionally, and started to act like a loser, not moving forward? Besides, God heard me. I refocused my attention on school and finishing as soon as possible. This was something I could control, something that gave me a distraction and a sense of reality apart from the fact that my kidneys were falling apart.

Chapter 23:

COLLEGE CONTINUED

My undergraduate degree pursuit at Middle Tennessee State University (MTSU) took up most of my time now that my painting business has slowed down, I managed to find a part-time gig as a therapist. I began working for a program that concentrated on helping children two through seven years of age with behavioral challenges, some stemming from past abusive experiences. Later, I worked as an in-home autism behavioral therapist for families whose children, also two through seven, were on the spectrum.

As I was pursuing a Sociology minor in addition to a Bachelor's in Psychology, Dr. Roberts, who taught this class, was one of the main influential people in the sociology department of MTSU. He, coincidentally, helped to spark my future love for research and writing. Being a writer and researcher himself, I talked to him after class one day about trying to balance my workload, and asked if I could do an independent study to earn the grade for my Sociology minor. He paused for a moment, rubbed his head, then looked right at me in a serious but curious stare.

"Sure, that sounds good. You have the grades in my class. Make sure it is comprehensive." "Yes, Sir," I replied.

I attacked my comprehensive research paper like a military mission, with strategy, planning, focus, and determination. I delved into various areas of sociology and settled on Gerontological Sociology. This area pertained to the elderly and ecological developments affecting their environments and resulting social interactions. At the end of the semester, I turned my research paper in and received an A plus, earning a Sociology minor. Mathematics and science, however, were a hugely different story.

At the start of my second semester at MTSU, I felt pretty good, having done well in my first semester of classes. I had a thought that medicine was pretty interesting, and I might want to do something with it. The way the human body is designed, how it copes with diseases, and even the systems seemed intriguing to me. I changed my major from Psychology to Pre-Med, thinking I wanted to eventually apply to medical school.

Walking into the building where all the Pre-Med students took their core classes, I saw a bunch of zoned-out students sitting around in the halls muttering to themselves. "What the heck are they on?" I said to myself. There was an element of studious lethargy everywhere as I walked to Organic Chemistry.

This class was composed of lecture time and then a

few hours of lab where I joined several other students in a room, working out Chemistry problems with beakers, scales, and chemicals. There were a lot of us crammed into this little room, so it made it harder to concentrate.

I had a rude wakeup call as I started to work on formulas. As I started writing out the problems, I put them down on paper backwards. I was supposed to write down my answers based on the performed chemical analysis, and completely screwed it up.

I might as well have been learning an undiscovered foreign language. The word impossibility is too generous a term for what I was experiencing. Everything I was doing was wrong. I was frustrated, defeated, and helpless.

Writing down anything that made any sense was impossible. It was very frustrating as students all around me easily completed their work, and many left before I even finished my first set of formulas. What made all of it worse was that in the lecture hall, concentrating on anything the professor said was utterly futile.

Entering the lecture hall, I tried to sit in the front so as not to be distracted. That was useless, because no matter how hard I tried, I could not keep from getting bothered by noises that seemed to pop up from everywhere. The anxiety and attention issues I suffered through my high school years returned without warning, full force.

The clock on the wall made a ticking sound in my ears, making me very upset. I was more worried about stopping that freaking noise than focusing on what was being said. Students all over the room were smacking gum, sounding as if it bounced off the walls. One day, I decided that I was finished with it, turned around during a lecture, and told someone right behind me, "..stop the noise making with your ridiculous gum chewing!"

Pencils and pens tapping got under my skin, and more than once, I had to leave the classroom in the middle of a lecture to try to compose myself.

Because focusing in class was nonexistent, I could not remember facts applying to formula-solving issues in the lab. I did so badly, as did a few other students, that at the end of the semester, the professor changed the passing grade curve from a sixty to a fifty percent. It was a sheer miracle. To this day, I have no idea how I earned a fifty percent, but I was very grateful to receive a D minus in spite of everything that could have earned an F.

The professor did not know it, but I believed God turned his heart to help me pass. Otherwise, it would have reduced my GPA even more, having a negative snowball effect on earning my Bachelor's degree. Needless to say, I changed my major back to Psychology.

There were other required classes to graduate, such as higher mathematics. However, now battling with recurring bouts of anxiety, attention deficit, and nervous issues, focusing on the fundamentals of algebra was a failed attempt. Concepts and formulas twisted in my mind, and I could not make sense of any math whatsoever. I was very afraid of failing, but kept it bottled up.

Every day, my anxiety became worse, and manifested into talking out loud to myself between classes to ease my feelings. Not realizing when I was doing it, I saw people staring at me one afternoon in the courtyard, but I could not have cared less. Somehow, it helped me calm down while walking from class to class. I was that little preteen kid again, lost and alone in his little room, lining up his Hot Wheels to stay sane, in the middle of 24,000 students.

Because of my recurring ADHD and anxiety issues, I was given a letter from a doctor certifying my learning disabilities. Failing my math curriculum, my grade in Algebra was changed from an F to passing due to the letter verification. After all was said and done, I earned my bachelor's degree in 2005 with a double minor in Sociology and Speech and Theater. God's Grace was there to help me, but I had to humble myself, realizing I could not do certain things. Jesus helped me through this tough time, and I was very grateful for being able to complete my second degree with a B average.

I went on to complete a graduate degree in School Guidance Counseling in 2010, becoming certified in both kindergarten through eighth grade and ninth through twelfth grade. I had a 3.7 GPA for all of my schoolwork, higher than what I accomplished in my bachelor's and much higher than in high school. God gave me progressively more favor with instructors and administration, renewing my mind academically as I successfully pressed forward in my studies, as grades reflected it.

Throughout my academic career, I experienced a decrease in anxiety, fear of people, and wanting to be by myself, allowing Jesus to continually heal me from these nagging lifelong issues triggered by different situations. My ADHD became progressively better as I worked very hard by learning how to not let outside stimuli affect me and distract me from what I was doing. This took a while, but by diligence, counseling, prayer, and persistence, I drastically reduced distractions when I needed to focus. I called it a gradual miracle of growth and maturity.

My mother once said being saved does not solve my problems, nor does it mean my life or decisions when faced with struggles are going to be perfect or easy, but God will be there. By facing the circumstances and embracing the problem by faith as I walk through the struggles, God recreates everything for my good, as He did by reinventing academic abilities, bringing emotional and psychological healing, victory, and transformation. I learned that I have to go through the middle of the hard things to be supernaturally transformed by them. Either allow the process to revolutionize my life, or give in to the failure and despair of whatever negative actions, circumstances, or craziness may come.

Chapter 24:

DEFYING THE PAIN

The first time I experienced raw, nerve-unwinding, intense pain was while working in my first district as a school guidance counselor. At first, it started as a dull ache in my big toe, but over an hour, the pain intensified, causing it to turn a deep red and swell. The slightest wind outside would aggravate it, and wearing a shoe without grimacing from insane discomfort lasted several days. A few more months went by with no flare-ups, then the pain attacks started again with increased frequency, moving into my knees, ankles, and the rest of my toes.

As time went on, the suffering became worse. Areas

affected became extremely swollen and rigid, feeling like there was a mixture of fluid and gravel caught between my joints. I could barely set my foot down to support my weight or bend my knees during the inflammation, causing me to scream in agony.

The feeling was like, if I had to put it in some sort of words, a white-hot throbbing knife cutting through my joints with every single heartbeat. I tried ice, elevation, and exercise, but nothing worked. I even tried to stretch it, but the pain only increased.

It took several minutes to get into the car before going anywhere during these episodes. I had to take my leg, forcing my brain to take the pain and push my leg past the straight position, angling my body in such a way that forced my other leg to put my foot on the brake pedal. Then I pushed my seat back and somehow got the rest of my body in the driver's seat.

I had to drive with my hurting leg as straight as possible, using one foot for the brake and gas. I refused to let it defeat me. Sometimes, I had to put my left leg over the gear shift and drive like a mailman on the passenger side when I had an automatic transmission. It was ridiculous.

At work, I used crutches and a brace I had from an old knee injury, scuffling down the hallways. I fell a few times, and no one, not even the teachers, asked if I needed help. That was disappointing, since I was their counselor at all hours of the day, helping them with whatever needed to be addressed psychologically, socially, mentally, and strategically with school issues.

At that moment, I realized I was in it by myself. No one but God could help me when in his sovereign Glory, He decided to do so. More than once, I cried out to Him, pleading that the pain would go away, even for a minute. Sometimes I felt relief, but most of the time it did not dissipate.

Sleep was practically non-existent. I stayed up all night, praying Jesus would heal me, trying to adjust my ankle on top of the couch, positioning myself in the craziest of angles. When my knee hurt, well, there was nothing I could do. When both ankle joints were on fire, I crawled on my stomach into the bathroom, grabbed hold of the toilet, and pulled myself onto it to do my business.

I saw a physical therapist, but it was useless. As best they could assume, I had a nerve condition. Regardless, even if God never healed me, I believed I could overcome this obstacle like many others. Besides, I refused to lose any days at work, being that it was my first job as a school guidance counselor.

Persevering through bones and joints being on fire, God still gave me insight and wisdom. I developed programs, co-developed educational community gatherings, and remodeled learning, training, and research facilities in the two years I was there. The first thing I observed was how dated and archaic the counseling office had become. Nothing had been done in the way of organization, updating the databases, or expanding student resources.

These country kids were pretty far away from anything that resembled a civilized city. They lived over an hour from the nearest metropolis and needed to have a more contemporary counseling center, apart from the dated school. I started the process by throwing out tons of trash from previous counselors.

I painted the walls of the counseling office with color schemes designed to give the students a feeling of doing their work in a contemporary, modernized coffeehouse. The remodeling also gave students a special and familiar place to call their own, away from their drab classroom walls. Every aspect of my office was updated, including furniture, filing systems, and college and scholarship application facilities.

God continued to download visions and ideas, and I created them accordingly. The Quiet Cube was a research, study, and assignment room for students who had difficulty with distractions and noises, something I had experience with and would have wanted for myself. Special needs students, those with learning disabilities, and traditional students who needed a place unto themselves could request to use it. It also became a very effective room for all students and teachers who needed a space to conduct meetings.

The Scholarship Room was a personal treat for me to create for students. This facility had computers, electric typewriters, scholarship information and applications, and file cabinets full of community and nationwide college, technical school, and university contact and campus information. It had modular seating placement and materials to make notations and jot down important academic references while using the installed phones placed at the desks.

When I did manage to walk with both feet more or less without crutches, I went to the Army National Guard up the road and connected with one of the guys in charge there. The Staff Sergeant and I developed a hybrid training program where students who were interested in the military could go and get a mini-training day to see if joining the Armed Forces would be a career option after graduation. Being a veteran, this was right up my alley and made this one of my projects.

We even had a Humvee equipped with all the latest military gadgets come visit the school district a few times. Grades seven through twelve had their turn at riding in the heavily-reinforced vehicle, and commented how fun it was to feel the huge wheels roll over any obstacle. This was a great primer for those who might consider the military as an option after high school. Being that many of these students tended to lean towards tech school, the military provided another practical option.

I also created College Nights where representatives from schools and colleges all over the United States came, providing question and answer sessions. Institutions of all types handed out invaluable information to interested parents and students. I developed and hosted The College and Career Day (CC Day) held annually, where technical schools, clubs, public and private universities, military branches, and community colleges were brought together for a comprehensive, informational gathering. There was also a meet and greet between students, parents, administrators, and teachers after the CC Day.

Those two years at my first job were an incredible learning and growing experience, and one from which I gleaned invaluable lessons, applying them to many parts of my life. I learned that when I decided to push forward and step out in faith, God sustained me beyond my capabilities. There were days I could not put one foot in front of the other down the long hallway to my office because of the fire in my feet, ankles, and knees. I kept remembering that it ultimately was not about me, but about doing the job no matter what, for the sake of those kids' futures. This was not a responsibility I took lightly.

What resulted was clarity and purpose, yielding innovation and creativity I may not have otherwise discovered within myself, given to me from God. Despite throbbing joint agony, I kept marching in faith to the next task. There was no quit.

In 2012, I started counseling at another school, this time in a larger district. I was in charge of several hundred boys in the seventh and eighth grades, and co-counseled with another counselor who was over the teenage girls. The old school, made of solid granite and marble, was so large that the theater with a balcony above the auditorium was between the second and third floors. My leg pain was not as often at this point, but did pop up from time to time, making it difficult to walk up the several flights of stairs inside and outside of the main building.

Back when I ran a painting business during my graduate degree program, I discovered the gift of realizing what spatial elements were lacking. I also knew what aesthetics were needed to enhance and improve the overall quality and effective experience. Similarly, as a school counselor, I realized I had a real gift of perceiving what was needed in an organization or what was lacking in a person's learning and training experience within a given organization or corporate and business entity. In this case, it was an academic setting.

A person who now looked for improvement beyond the inevitable or obvious, I started to ask around and see what kind of opportunities were available to students for after-school, extracurricular activities, and student improvement programs and events. The girls had the cooking club, sewing club, and a host of other clubs keeping them engaged aside from schoolwork. The young men had nothing to engage in that helped them broaden their knowledge base beyond the academic curriculum, outside of class time.

With permission from the school district, I developed some helpful scholastic programs. The Carpe Diem Club for Boys was a scientific research and activity-integrated after-school program that helped to engage boys in rudimentary, scientific principles of flight, aerodynamics, and mechanics. Organizational Bootcamp helped to improve the overall placement and accessibility of school supplies, books, and materials through daily accountability of locker and study material organization.

Being a patriot and Navy veteran, I wanted to maintain and improve the observance of Veterans' Day. The Veteran's Day Assembly Program did just this. As a school, we honored local veterans and respected the United States Flag by having a local Boy Scout troop perform a color guard March, and other patriotic presentations.

One of the primary mandates put in place by the district and the state to educate students about certain subjects and ideals about education was a presentation about not bullying in schools. Hence, I developed and presented the Anti-Bullying Campaign. I discovered that by combining a visual and interactive approach to learning about bullying, the residual side effects were quite effective for the student body.

Students were always a priority, and I always made it a point to ensure a safe and secure place in my office. Students and their parents knew I was their advocate. But then, out of nowhere, a nightmare happened.

As a school counselor, there were times when students came to my office for rewards and encouragement, but sometimes holding serious group sessions between the student, teacher, and I were necessary. These were more of an overall assessment and mini-intervention concerning grades, behavior, and/or a student's home life. They could be one-on-one or in a group setting, depending on the issue and situation presenting itself. I enjoyed helping my students through difficult times and made it all worthwhile, especially when they realized positive changes within themselves.

In this particular case, a student was having trouble keeping his behavior in check during classroom work time, mocking someone, and displaying defiant issues apart from the usual teenage antics. I decided to call him into my office. After speaking with him, I had his parents join us at our next meeting to get a sense of the kind of home life he had and what might be causing him to react in class when certain emotional triggers presented themselves.

I asked some open-ended questions about their child, like whether they had experienced any oppositional or blatantly defiant types of behavior that were out of the usual norm at home. We talked for a little while, exchanging some information about the student. These two parents seemed very caring and were open to working with me and their child to see what was going on, and help as a team to address and improve behaviors. Then, I called the classroom where the student was located, asking the teacher to have the student meet us in my office.

When the student walked into my office, it was the wrong one. And it was not his fault, it was mine. Somehow, I mixed up the names of the boy and the parents.

To make matters worse, I had given a long story of how their son was acting in school and with other students. I was convinced that I had not confused any of this, but I did. I just sat there when these parents told me this was not their son.

This scared family became very concerned that I either lost their boy or I was wasting their time. Either way, this was a screwed up situation that quickly escalated. For clarity, this was a school district that prided itself on helping and caring for, as they indicated, undocumented children and their families. If any mistake was unwillingly caused by one student, even if they were legitimately wrong in their behaviors, the teachers and administrators were usually the first ones to be questioned, and usually accused.

This district, which was very open and accepting of minorities, was one of the main reasons I chose to work there. I embraced the challenge of working with a multicultural school. But because I somehow mismatched a student and parents, the principal quickly heard about it, and I was summoned by her, saying what I did was essentially unforgivable. Seemingly, the very same school district that forgave and went out of its way to understand and accommodate those who showed up in America for help could not do the same for its committed employees.

I tried to ease the principal's concerns, explaining that somehow, uncharacteristically, I mixed up the student with the wrong parents, and the principal became very angry at me. Even though I was fully open, transparent, and ready to accept constructive criticism, it was not adequate for her. I assured her the issue was resolved and we took care of their child, emphasizing it would never happen again.

Seeing that I was not getting through, I was immediately judged as having made a grave mistake that ill-represented her school district. I walked back in the next morning and put in my resignation, telling her I would be leaving at the end of the school year. If I tried to beg, I may have just given her more reasons to fire me, citing weakness of character. Hence, the best way was to cut my losses and move on, letting God take care of my future and redeem me from that confused mess.

Leaving that school district seemed to work out just fine, but there was a lingering nagging about why I did such a stupid thing. Everything about this event was more than a simple case of paperwork misfiled or unorganized. I felt like there was some kind of foggy confusion in my head. I was usually mentally and physically sharp, knowledgeable, and knew everything in-depth about my counseling role, so none of it made any sense to me.

As I was finishing up my time at that school district, I reflected on my circumstances and how everything unfolded. It did suck that I was treated so poorly, but I chose to see it as God opening the door to pursue my doctorate full-time. I would soon learn this is also what faith is all about, seeing past the inevitable.

Chapter 25:

DOCTORATE PURSUIT

It was Christmas break, 2012. I was visiting some friends at their home when the wife of my buddy started to talk about her doctorate, and how it was through Lindenwood University. It was an accelerated, three-year doctoral track located in Missouri. I told her I had been researching colleges about their doctorate offerings, and the fact that she had started hers piqued my interest.

She said to check out Lindenwood because they had a great, year-round program, attending classes with no breaks. The catch was that this was New Year's Eve, and classes started back up in the first week of January. She said I may not be able to start, but contact the regional director as soon as possible to see when the next round of candidates begins.

Deciding I would not take no for an answer, I found out who the regional director of the program was and contacted him. He and I soon met, and after about half an hour, I was miraculously allowed to start my doctorate in January 2013 without any prerequisite testing, entrance exam, or wait time. God had made a way for me to start on time, without any administrative delay, just days after I found out about the program.

The hands-on teaching, collaboration, and integrative work styles of this accelerated doctorate were made for my particular style of learning. The curriculum took an average of seven years for traditional doctorate programs and condensed it into a three-year time frame. I found that this accelerated, "pressure cooker" approach to assimilating information worked well for my brain, and I was set to process the workload with speed and efficiency better than any other school work I had done in the past.

Make no mistake, the crazy way that this advanced doctoral curriculum packed seven average years of doctoral-level coursework into three years' worth of dissertation topic development, research, and class work was insane. The pace at which I was to be challenged to perform by the professors was nuts, but I found that I thrived in a borderline ecstatic state of stress, much like in the Navy technical training program.

Similarly, I worked very well under pressure. God had set me up for this academic moment, specifically designed from way back in my early years, coupled with the discipline from the military. I decided to stop working until I completed school, after counseling for three years in two different districts. I did what practically every other doctoral student does in America: took out as many student loans as possible and lived on them. It was a great decision because school took twelve to sixteen hours a day, minimum, for research, studying, and class assignments. Social activities and going out on dates were few and far between, and so was my joint pain. I did work out and try to keep myself physically in shape, and overall fitness in check. I finally found a good balance between all of it, and seeing that I could balance the many things in my life helped me to see that I could live a pretty normal existence. Life was going well until it took an unforeseen turn, one that changed every aspect of my life forever.

Defying the Lies: A Memoir

Chapter 26:

MY SUPERHERO HAS CANCER

Dad's voice was somber, laced with sadness and hurt. I sensed he was upset, trying to hide something. I asked him what was going on that made him feel so bad.

Like several times before, Mom had been walking her usual five miles down the sidewalk of their neighborhood. She came into the front yard when dad was coming out the front door, looked at her, and noticed that her eyes seemed glossy, the whites of her eyes yellow. He knew something was not right, and they immediately called the doctor.

They quickly drove to the hospital. A thorough workup revealed her liver was not working very well, and doctors had to find out why it went from good to bad in a short while. A few days later, they both found out mom's condition was a lot worse than they initially assumed.

Mom was diagnosed with pancreatic cancer located in the center of the organ, and it was growing aggressively. According to the doctors who were located in one of the top two cancer research hospitals in the United States, Mom's prognosis was that without immediate treatment, she would be dead in a matter of a few months.

According to her cancer doctor, who happened to be one of the top pancreatic cancer doctors in the United States, Mom's type was one of the most aggressive and least treatable cancers in existence. To have any chance of survival, her doctors and the surgeon recommended beginning chemotherapy to shrink the tumor, followed by surgery. Mom and Dad opted to start immediately on treatment.

After dad told me all of this information, I slowly hung up the phone and sank onto the floor in stunned silence. My mother, who was always healthy and looked upon by others as a super mom, was suddenly thrust into a situation that impacted everyone she knew. A woman who was healthier than many of her peers was now in the fight of her life.

But why did this woman, who was practically a saint and a huge advocate of helping others succeed despite her own needs and desires, now have cancer? Why was she chosen to face this horrible, venerable enemy straight from hell? She was a mom's mom and a child's greatest hero, loving beyond realization or circumstance. My mind began drifting to memories of just how incredible she was.

Mom was an amazing athlete even in high school. At

only five feet three inches, her peers said she was a short but huge bundle of energy all over the high school basketball court. Newspapers and reporters who kept up with high school sports, from all over, said how amazing her athletic career was because she was so fast and reliable in the game. She earned her place on the all-state Louisiana basketball team and was revered as one of the best all-time athletes of her high school because of her amazing three-pointers.

Growing older, Mom tried to take care of herself. Sure, the Cajun food she cooked was delicious, amazing, and probably not the best for her body, but Mom was always aware of staying in shape. She loved walking and loved to do things outdoors. Mom was also an unreal motorcycle rider who could manage the snowy Cascade mountains and valleys with the best of them.

Mom was also a person who self-sacrificed and looked after her children through the hardest of times. When we were very young and dad barely made any money, mom went without food for days so my brother and I could eat. When there was nothing in the cabinets or refrigerator, she did what had to be done to protect her babies.

Being an incredible writer, she won several awards in school for her essays. I found a few examples of them tucked away in a drawer and asked Mom when she wrote them. She smiled and said that was a long time ago, but she always wondered what would have happened if she had pursued her dreams. I guess submitting to dad and whatever he wanted was more important than using her gifts and talents. To this day, I do not understand why.

From talking to her, I could tell Mom wanted to do something with her talent in writing. She was, however, resolute in doing whatever her present life dictated, that being service to her family. She swallowed her wants and accepted Dad's constant traveling requirements. Rarely was it out of her control, but nevertheless, she followed his direction with faithfulness despite her personal needs. I did inherit that writing talent from her, and when I do, I often think of my superhero.

She was a selfless person who did not care about personal needs and often went without in many areas. When we moved, she would get rid of things that Dad told her could not be packed for the trip. I think it was a real shame she never realized her fullest potential in this life, but things do happen for a reason. My brother and I may have never been born, and I would not be writing this book.

Mom always had a huge smile for my brother and me, arms to cry in, and a heart to love her children through the sorrows and pain we were experiencing growing up. These selfless acts were repeated several times over the years. She would do what had to be done to make sure, in spite of all the moving and transitions, that I was safe, even emotionally. Sometimes, that meant dancing.

I caught mom dancing and praising God in the kitchen more than once, coming in to eat before school. Mom was so energetic and happy when she was praising God, dancing, and loving life as she prepared eggs, bacon, and grits on many a day. This helped to encourage me when everything seemed upside down and hopeless, at least for the time being. She laughed and loved life and loved her Savior, Jesus Christ.

Speaking of cooking, Mom made the best fried chicken anywhere. All of her friends would ask for the recipe of that scrumptiously fried delicacy, including hamburgers, gumbo, spaghetti and meatballs, and fried catfish. Man, those spaghetti and meatballs; I can taste them right now. On Sundays, Mom started very, very early in the morning, right when she woke up. She started with fresh vegetables, carefully chopping and slicing them up exactly and perfectly, so they would cook properly and look right in the sauce when it was poured over spaghetti.

Yes, that infamous sauce. Mom took hours to methodically prepare the thick, red, sweet, and spicy concoction bubbling up in her iron pot, cooking slowly on the stove. What went into the many ingredients is still not precisely known, adding to the mystery of Mom's unbelievable cooking. I still have not discovered her recipe, and that is just fine with me.

Finally, the homemade spaghetti noodles gently covered by that amazing tomato succulence were hand-formed. The counter was dusted with flour, then Mom broke out the eggs, butter, and all the other ingredients, mixing and kneading the dough in just the right way. Then she used a noodle strainer to create long, skinny strands, and cooked them in a way that produced the best spaghetti and meatballs I have ever eaten. Ever.

As if there was anything else to praise mom for, there was her relentless, sheer will when facing horrible circumstances. We were taking care of some foster children when I was around eleven, and I became locked out of the house. Well, knowing that the keys were inside, mom tried to open a sliding glass window to the kitchen, but it broke in a jagged "V". Her arm slid down the sharp edge, stopping at the bottom of the pane of glass. It sliced her arm to the bone, leaving nothing else to hold the skin, tissue, and ligaments together.

Quickly grabbing her arm with blood gushing from the arteries and veins, she ran over to the neighbor's house and was rushed to the hospital. After several hours of life-saving surgery, mom was put into a cast with rubber bands sewn through her fingernails to keep the tendons from shortening and causing permanent damage to the nerves. Mom went through several months of horrendous physical therapy, including her entire arm being dipped in hot wax. Then she had to attempt to close her fist while in excruciating pain, every tendon forced to move and stretch through the developing scar tissue, keeping it broken loose and pliable. Mom never cried once.

Despite dealing with her recovery, trying to be there for her family, and now nurturing three foster siblings, she refused to let any of it go. Mom blatantly, despite dad's pleas, flat-out refused to let those neglected children be put back into the system. She loved them so much that her comfort was secondary to their well-being and success.

After sitting on the floor in stupefied shock for what seemed like an hour, I began pleading to God, asking Him not to let this be true. I could not believe that my mother, also a teacher and special needs instructor for decades, and unconditional lover of her family, had cancer. How could this be?

I called dad back and told him I was jumping in the car, but he said not to come yet because they were trying to schedule doctor appointments and calling everyone to pray for her. I did not understand this because Mom needed her "baby boy" with her. She was always there for me, and I wanted to be there for her.

Nevertheless, Dad insisted on waiting until they had

things worked out, and to this day, I question Dad's decision and my response. I should have insisted and gotten my butt down there as soon as possible to help the family out. Anyway, I called my girlfriend and told her the bad news. She was upset for me, and I needed her by my side, but because of work, she could not take time off to fly down just yet.

I kept tabs on mom, calling her often and driving down once in a while to see her. Thankfully, she was responding very well to treatments and was praised by her doctors for how well she was doing. My family and friends rejoiced because we saw God really working on mom's behalf.

She was her happy, bubbly self, acting like nothing was different apart from a port in her chest for the chemo drip. It was awesome to see her responding so well and fighting through all of it with her giant-sized faith. In fact, mom's hair never fell out, and she never felt sick after chemo treatments. The doctors had no explanation, but I certainly did. God received all the credit for these miracles.

Mom finished her chemo treatments, and the cancer in her pancreas had shrunk enough for the doctors to go in and remove the rest of it. The surgeons had to perform a very invasive Whipple surgery to ensure all of the cancer was removed, but we all had high hopes and were happy that Mom was doing well. Overall, she was on her way to being cancer-free, and God would receive all the credit.

My girlfriend and I made a trip to see Mom after her surgery in Atlanta because we wanted to find out about the results. She was also a very experienced military and civilian surgical anesthetist and nurse, and could ask the right questions and get better explanations from mom's care team. We arrived in town, and after checking in at the hotel, drove to the hospital.

My brother and his family were in the room with us, visiting with Mom. All of my nieces and nephews were purposefully distracted, running around and having fun in the halls of the hospital. It was a happy reprieve away from the seriousness. Family being present helped mom's demeanor, and all were encouraged to hear her doing well after surgery. Overall, she was on her way to improving, and we were told she was on her way to beating pancreatic cancer survival rate statistics.

The resident surgical expert on pancreatic cancer told us they took out everything they could get, and now it was time to wait and see what happened. We all talked about alternatives to future treatment. My girlfriend asked some great in-depth questions as well, clarifying puzzling issues we encountered, and helped to answer questions presented by the surgeons and my family. A family plan was also developed moving forward, and all of the issues associated with mom's cancer treatment began getting fleshed out. After saying goodbye, we returned home, having an overall sense that Mom's cancer prognosis would continue to improve.

I knew God was in control of my family, regardless of how things looked in the past or present. This also meant this cancer fight. Even though I had doubt and sadness, I knew God was the ultimate healer, however it came about.

Chapter 27:

SIGNS OF LIFE

Resigning from a school district, moving to a new city, pursuing my doctorate, and my mom being diagnosed with pancreatic cancer all in the same year made life unrealistically hectic and mentally challenging. But like everything else previously encountered, there came the choice of giving up or pushing through it. My faith in God gave me supernatural strength, and I acted on it. Sometimes I felt as if everything was piling up at times, and people would ask me how I would keep going on and on through it all. Smiling, I would simply say, "I choose to."

In 2013, we had some really warm temperatures, and it was a time to get out and enjoy some summer fun. I was looking forward to swimming, running, and doing my best to glean from Missouri's usually beautiful weather. But contrary to the feelings of summer warmth on my face, I noticed that despite what I was supposed to experience hanging out on the deck and swimming in the pool, I was oddly cold when I jumped out of the water, despite temperatures in the high 90s.

My usual summer practice was to crank up the air-conditioning in my car and the thermostat in my apartment down to stay cool. But I was puzzled, because it was not necessary. I started to turn up the heat in the middle of summer in my car and apartment. The fact that my body was telling me one thing and the environment something else made no sense at all.

By August, I found myself increasing my apartment's temperature to stay warm. I constantly had the feeling of standing in the middle of a deep freeze. It turned into an all-day, ever-increasing issue. I wore sweaters and thick clothing despite the bright and warm sun. My hands always felt cold, and I stopped sweating, even during intense workouts.

For the next three or four months, I started to urinate a lot. When I say a lot, I mean fourteen to fifteen times a day. I could not stay very long at church, nor plan to stay anywhere for any length of time. Frothy bubbles, later known as excessive protein spillage, showed up in my urine upon landing in the toilet. It had been occurring for several months, but I ignored it.

Before any thoughts of physical illness crept into my mind, I quickly stifled them and went about my business. Eventually, I could no longer ignore these physical signs, because now the itching had started. And man, it was beyond insane.

On January 14, 2014, I started to feel intensely itchy all over my body, and no amount of scratching stopped it. My mind was fuzzy, like in a semi-sleep state, but moving in slow motion. I called up my brother and told him what was going on.

He told me I should go to the hospital immediately. I said I would wait a bit longer to see how I felt. I did not want to admit what I thought was happening to me, because after all the years fighting and fending off the inevitable, it was most probably coming to fruition. This was not the right time for any of this.

I could not sleep that night. Excruciating itching plagued my body. My brain was fogged up with confusion, and I had not been sweating for months. Now, my body was sweating so much my sheets were soaked, and I was even colder.

Early, before the sun came up, I made a call to a long-time friend and explained my situation. I could no longer put off getting help and told her that what was happening to me was getting worse. She also told me to go to the hospital as fast as possible.

She helped me go through my checklist of things to take to the hospital. This was a simple way to make me stay focused because by now, even remembering my name was not going to happen. Together, we found my jeans, shirt, boots, money, and wallet. Man, I was glad to have her on the other end of the line.

It took me several minutes to get everything together, and longer to start organizing the apartment before I left. My friend got onto me for trying to get everything neat before leaving. The next thing I had to do, because no one was around to do so, was to drive to the hospital.

Yeah, it was crazy to say the least. Why I did not call an ambulance is still a mystery to me. I still cannot remember driving to the emergency room.

The next thing I knew, I was getting out of my car,

and the cold January air was hitting me right in the chest. I stumbled through the emergency room doors, and before I said anything, I saw people at the front desk staring at me like something was wrong. I told one of the nurses the best way I could that I was itching beyond belief, feeling like I was delirious, and freezing. She told me to sit down to the side of the desk, then asked who drove me. I said I drove myself, and was met with wide-eyed disbelief. It was truly a miracle that I even remembered how to get to the hospital.

My temperature and blood pressure were taken. Before I could ask the nurse what it said, someone appeared out of nowhere with a bed on wheels, then nurses and some other people put me onto that gurney, pushed me through a large set of wooden doors, and took me to the back. As I was being taken down the long hallway that connected the front waiting room to the back emergency patient rooms, I bent my neck and noticed many, many different people who were injured and sick, waiting in seats and also on gurneys, all the way down on each side of the hallway.

I was puzzled. Why were there all these people waiting for a doctor when I was immediately taken back? I saw some people out of the corner of my eye who were bleeding and in pain. They looked at me, and I still remember the look on their faces. I barely mumbled to the guy who was pushing me back, "Why me?" He said that the hospital makes sure patients who are in critical condition get pushed back first. I dropped my head on the pillow and closed my eyes.

I was wheeled into a room by myself, and the nurse put an IV into my arm. Everything seemed just fine, regardless of what was going on around me. It was weird because I had no anxiety, fear, or worry.

I could sense that Jesus was with me in the room and had a clearer head than when I was at home. Others came into the room and took blood from me, took my temperature, and asked how I was feeling. I thought I was doing okay, but the behavior and actions of the doctors and nurses said something else. I had a peace amid that storm, and knew no matter what happened to me, I was going to be okay. I had learned this during near-fatal aircraft malfunctions while flying to New Zealand.

I called my brother again and told him I was at the hospital in the emergency room, but not to worry because I was just getting a checkup to make sure I was alright. I believed that in the face of everything I was experiencing, it was going to be just fine. I called dad and told him the same. Dad was taking care of Mom and could not come, but my brother said he was on the way.

If it was my time to go home to Heaven and be with Jesus, not having to deal with any more struggles, pain, or disappointment in this life, then I was completely okay with it. I had peace in that hospital bed, and nothing the doctors could tell me would distract me from this fact. I knew I was ready to go home to be with the Lord, being more sure of this than anything else.

In a matter of hours, I was quickly prepped for transport to the Columbia, Missouri, veteran hospital facility, a few hours away. The ambulance people loaded me up, and we took off. On the way, an old pain crept back into the joint and under the kneecap of my right knee.

It started as a dull pricking, perhaps because I was restrained, keeping my legs from moving too much. I told the ambulance EMT who was monitoring my vitals about my leg, and she just said Try to keep it as still as possible. Did she not understand the level of pain I was having, requiring constant readjustment of my knee joint?

When we arrived, I was put into a room with another person for a few hours, then by myself because the nurse realized I was going to be a kidney dialysis patient. Earlier, on the phone call with my brother, I told him where I was headed so he could meet me there after whatever they were going to do to me. Before I left for Columbia, I briefly posted on social media what was going on, asking friends and family to pray during this ordeal.

My little brother arrived in Colombia a few hours after I did, and it was perfect timing. He was a God-send, taking care of health insurance, living will, advance directives, and other pertinent paperwork. The veteran's hospital needed many things to process me into the hospital as a patient, more than I could have ever done for myself. I could not have had a better ally.

As we were talking, my knee that had started to mildly hurt in the ambulance began throbbing with every heartbeat. I somehow bent my leg the wrong way, and it sent a surge of tremendous white-hot pokers right through the center of it. I screamed out and grabbed it, turning and writhing in the bed. No matter which way I moved my leg, the pain just became worse. I began pleading with the nurses to get me something for the pain, but they did not seem to hear.

Cursing at the top of my lungs, pissed off and mad at everyone in that room, I yelled out, "Why is everyone ignoring me!" Then, as if God knew exactly what I needed, a friend from when I was a teenager walked right into the room and grabbed my hand. Like an angel appearing out of nowhere, he walked to the side of my bed, grabbed my hand with both of his, and started praying the pain would go away.

I cried out to God as he prayed. I do not remember how long he stayed in that room, but as mysteriously as he arrived, he left. If I did not know who he was, I would have thought he was an angel sent for that exact moment in time.

Eventually, they gave me prednisone, and the pain quickly stopped. Come to find out through all of this, doctors told me these painful attacks in my joints were the buildup of uric acid in my body, called Gout, the by-products of certain foods. My failing kidneys could not filter out this waste chemical, so it settled and crystallized inside my joints. It was rocks of solidified uric acid grinding into my kneecap from beneath, and between my joints. With the amount of agony experienced in the slightest movement, I would have settled for having my leg cut off.

Even though he was a tremendous help, my brother did have it rough. He witnessed me behaving in ways that I was not normally, often yelling and cursing at nurses because of the steroids given to me. Even in stressful situations, I had never reacted so horrendously. I became so crazy that he needed to occasionally walk out of the room.

In his defense, I was often demanding and insistent about needing pain medication, or food, or any number of things that would come up. The high levels of steroids made me irritated and short-tempered, and a person whom people did not want to be around. A doctor came into my room saying they were going to prep me for an emergency heart catheterization for kidney dialysis. I told them flat out, somehow now being able to talk clearly, that I did not want to remember or feel anything. I was given some medicine, and the next thing I knew, I was being quickly wheeled back through a maze of freezing hallways.

As I entered the operating room, a nurse with a large smile on her face lifted up a package that had long, coiled up plastic tubing in it. She said this was going to be put into my chest to help me. To this day, I think this was an uncharacteristically odd way to tell a patient what was going to be put into their chest. She was so weirdly happy about it, acting like I won an all-expenses-paid vacation anywhere. Truth be told, I was probably stoned out of my mind from the meds.

The next thing I remember, I woke up in a room with tubes sticking out of the right side of my upper chest with fittings at the ends of them. The tubing stuck out about five inches from where it entered my body. It was split into a V-shaped connector, which was two separate pieces of plastic tubing with taped fittings on the ends.

This central venous catheter (CVC) was a long, plastic tube with two small plastic anchors sewn onto the skin of my chest. From there, it was pushed through my right jugular vein, down, and then curved left across my chest cavity into the top right atrium of my heart. The surgeon later told me that the CVC was an emergency procedure that could be used as soon as it was placed, and was the most effective and quickest way to dialyze my blood.

The doctors told me that my blood urea number (BUN) showed a Nitrogen level of ninety-nine milligrams, whereas a normal range is about seven to eighteen milligrams. In short, my kidneys were ceasing to function. This level was around ten times as much as my body could manage. The dangerously high level of Nitrogen had flooded my body, causing extreme itching, confusion, and foggy delirium. Jesus kept me alive until the surgeons stabilized my vitals, making a way when there was no way.

I found out later that my creatinine level was 8.7, when a normal range for a typical human being is less than 1.0, going down into the hundredths place of the decimal range. Furthermore, my body was in extreme dehydration, indicating that the systems of my body were starving for water and shutting down. Lastly, I was told that the average human being has between sixty and eighty liters of blood an hour being cleaned by both kidneys, every second of one's life.

For reference, that is enough blood to fill sixty to eighty one-liter-sized soda bottles. However, my kidneys only had seven liters of blood an hour being cleaned. God kept me alive as I believed by faith. He had everything in control.

That meant that between both of my kidneys, they could no longer filter out the impurities, slowly building up dangerous levels of toxins over the years. My body could no longer get rid of the deadly by-products. Both kidneys had turned to mostly scar tissue and were no longer doing their jobs. I was also told that I should have been checked out three years ago and could have been put on dialysis.

Within an hour after surgery, I was taken to another area right around the corner from my room. There, I was introduced to the machine that kept me alive and at the same time, cost me everything. I sat in the red chair with the electronic tower of lights, buttons, and sounds to my right. The nurse took a few clear hoses hanging from what looked like a long car oil filter in a clear tube, hooked them up to the leads sticking out of my chest, and started up the kidney dialysis machine by pressing a few buttons.

Watching blood flow out of my body from one tube and into this invention of rescue, the dialyzer made this sort of soft swishing and clicking noise. The interior electronics, sensors, wiring, relays, and wheel mechanisms spun and made the blood go through the machine, getting the impurities out. Once the blood was filtered with certain chemicals, it returned to the other plastic tube.

I just sat there in awe, staring at the electronics. I did not know what to think, do, or even feel. Throughout the entire week, I stayed dialyzed to make sure my blood ratios were as normal as possible. Because of kidney dialysis, I had to be careful how much water I consumed because my body, according to the nephrologists and nurses, held onto it.

The first time I was hooked up to the dialysis machine in Columbia, I got sick to my stomach. I called out to the attending dialysis nurses running all over the place, helping several patients in the treatment room, but before anyone heard me, I passed out. Next thing I knew, I was lying flat on my dialysis chair and had five nurses talking and nudging me to wake up.

That freaked me out, man. I had no idea what just happened, crying like a big baby, and was disoriented. This nice nurse bent over and softly told me that I had passed out and everything would be just fine. Come to find out, I prematurely hit my target weight based on weigh-ins, becoming completely dehydrated. This weight is set on the dialysis machine to get the patient to the lowest bodyweight possible as fluid is drawn out of the blood, before passing out, but no one expected this anomaly.

Kidney dialysis patients gain an average of ten to fifteen pounds of fluid over one day, in between treatments. So I was being treated as if I had at least ten pounds of extra fluid in my blood, every other day. But miraculously, I never, ever gained any fluid, and in fact always weighed like a normal person having two fully-functioning kidneys.

So when food came around, I defied the obvious, asking if I could substitute some of it for water. Then I worked the system and got as much water as possible, even if it meant starving to death. Water was something I craved, and I would do anything to get it.

This was unexplainable by my doctors and nurses, but I knew how to explain it. God was with me, and Jesus helped me overcome impossible physical odds through a creative miracle, just like many other supernatural times in my life. Once the nurses set the kilograms for my bodyweight and stopped the machine from taking off any water weight, I was good to go. After I was deemed stable enough to return home, my brother drove me back, and it was a great trip. We caught up and joked about crazy stuff we did as kids, and enjoyed our time together.

Chapter 28:

KIDNEY DIALYSIS LIFE

I woke up bleary-eyed the morning after I arrived back home. I dressed, made an egg and some toast, crawled into my car half-awake, and headed out across town for my first dialysis treatment outside of the hospital. It was eerily quiet that morning. The soft revving of my car's engine between gearshifts and the soft, low buzzing of the worn-out heater fan were the only noises I heard, driving through that cold, quiet city.

Cars were sparsely parked in dimly lit parking lots of businesses, dotting the edges of the highway. I thought about what these people might be doing or where they were, and what they had done over the weekend. It must have been anything better than what I was experiencing. Their realities were far from mine, and I was already jealous of what they could do, whenever they could do it.

The roads and highways were empty, skeletons of

asphalt roadways lining the hilly cityscape. For the first time in a very long time, before I could remember when, my mind was clearer, able to focus on what I was thinking. Man, my body must have been screwed up.

 I decided to drive slowly through the downtown area and realized that I was finally seeing it with a healthy perspective; literally. I could not remember when everything seemed this bright, vivid, and tactile. I made my way to the north side, up a bit further on the highway, then turned onto a side service road and drove into the DaVita treatment facility. It had been an old Blockbuster video rental store until all of them across the United States started going out of business due to movies going digital and online.

 This was a bittersweet memory of things long past. Much like seeing videocassette recorder tapes being replaced with DVDs, my life was changed in ways I never expected. I pulled into a handicapped parking space, shut the car off, and saw people hooked up to their machines as I walked inside.

 I was the only one in the waiting area at five-fifteen in the morning. There were wiped-down tables and chairs like you would find in any typical doctor's office or hospital waiting room. The television on the wall was on low, playing the morning news. I zoned out watching the person talk about morning traffic until a few minutes later, a nurse with a happy demeanor opened the door, snapping me back to reality. She called out my name, and I followed her back through the door to the main treatment area.

 The first thing I did was to complete a weigh-in, removing everything from my pockets, my coat, and anything that might make me weigh more than the digital printout depicted. The weight machine looked more like something a shipping station would use. My weight came in the form of kilograms. By the way, I became pretty good at reading and understanding this form of measurement, being that I had to weigh myself every day before and after treatment.

I made my way across the floor with the nurse leading me through a maze of several dialysis machines similar to what I saw back in the hospital. Some patients were sleeping while others were watching their televisions attached to the sides of their dialysis chairs. I was met with several reddened and tired eyes staring at me as I walked to my dialysis machine.

I was led to a solitary space with glass walls at the far corner of the room, where new dialysis patients were put to be closely monitored. The chair was set in one corner, the dialysis machine being nearby. The setup of the chairs, nurse's stations, and dialysis machines around the outside perimeter of the unit was also similar to the ones in Columbia. The nurse took my temperature with a band-type mechanism, then took my standing and seated blood pressure.

My nurse removed the taped-on gauze covering the entryway of the emergency chest catheter. Then she took fresh gauze soaked in some type of clear antibacterial disinfectant fluid that smelled like denatured alcohol, and began scrubbing where the tubes went into my chest. This raw area was already sensitive to touch and movement, so as the three days a week hemodialysis procedure began, I was introduced to a different type of pain that made me jump out of my chair. When I say they cleaned my chest catheter area, this is a gross understatement.

Blood, pus, and fluid from inside my body would

normally leak out and surround the access every few days, causing some scabbing around the chest tube. Because it was an exposed opening to the inside of my body, the entire wound area needed to be thoroughly sterilized. Using scissors, excess scabs were cut from the wound.

Scrubbing around the chest tube, all remaining foreign debris was removed. What made it worse was that I had a hairy chest, so it all got stuck on that. I still find myself rubbing my chest where the tube was inserted, remembering how bad it was. I had to take whatever came and roll with it. Either this, or die.

This anti-bacterial scrubbing procedure helped to ensure the exposed hole with the tube inside of it did not let any foreign bodies or deadly bacteria get inside my body. If this happened, a fast infection could kill me by bacteria following the tube through the artery into my heart. Pain told me I was alive, so I sucked it up and took it. After a few months, the hole did close properly and attach itself via scar tissue to the end of the port as expected, which made these thrice weekly, six-hour dialysis routines a little less unnerving.

Living off a machine, I had to be extremely careful. Any kind of germ or bacteria could kill me. Shower water creeping into the chest access tube, dirt on my skin from sweat or picking something up in a public place could result in an emergency trip to the hospital. There were many instances when the site might become infected, even from walking outside and not remembering to wear a shirt.

Some random particle of dust getting lodged next to, or inside the wound, could have also started an infection that could have spread, and then it would be lights out.

Let me tell you, after the very first cleaning procedure, I made sure that the nurse cleaned the incision area as well as possible. But contrary to my pleas of taking it easy on me, the nurses insisted on what I had come to know as a pure evil process of cutting, scrubbing, cleaning, and redressing my chest catheter site.

After a wound dressing, I was hooked up to the machine, and the nurse who was assigned to me drew blood from one of my access tubes to later measure the pre-treatment levels of fluid, poisons, blood platelets, waste, mineral levels, and others. Then injections prepared in advance were administered into my dialysis machine via tubes with special needle ports. Bags were hanging from IV hooks like you would normally see in the hospital for saline in case I needed some during treatment, and I sometimes needed it. Remember, I never retained fluid.

Total dependence on the nurses and the dialysis process was now my normal daily practice. My very existence depended on three days a week, four-hour dialysis treatments. This machine of modern miracles was my computerized, mechanical, and hydraulic kidney, keeping my blood healthy enough to ensure I could stay alive. I was sometimes issued prednisone if I had a gout attack, but after a few months, I seldom had them. Unfortunately, the machine barely removed the urea and uric acid levels during dialysis, as it only purified 5 to 10 percent of my blood during a treatment.

Food became a necessity for fuel and staying alive to thrive, and not for entertainment, comfort, or even taste. Nutrition became a tool, nothing more. I made superfood shakes from vegetables and fruits, all uncooked. I cooked chicken, but no red meat, because it had purines that caused gout. I even had a few friends convert to smoothie lovers. Others became more open to the idea of eating their fruits and vegetables more healthily.

I stayed away from nuts, legumes, ice cream, and anything with multigrain or whole grain oats because these foods also contained purines that could create uric acid. It was mandatory if I wanted to stay healthy, but now and then, I hated not being able to eat whatever I wanted. I chose to stay as healthy as possible in spite of my cravings. After a while, I no longer wanted the foods I used to eat, like ice cream and steak. None of it was appetizing to me.

Due to being on kidney dialysis, I was immunosuppressed, meaning my body could not aggressively fight disease like everyone else's. I had to be extremely careful where I went, who I was with, and what I exposed myself to in the natural environment because germs and bacteria were my mortal enemies. I wore a mask when I became sick or if I knew I would be around many people, because any contact might affect me more than the average healthy person.

Going to any place that had crowds of any size was very hazardous, and staying away from any opportunity to be in contact with a group larger than ten. This constant, acute awareness of germs made me a germaphobe, constantly washing my hands and walking quickly away from others who tried to get close to me. Running across friends in public venues was awkward and uncomfortable, to say the least.

I had to keep my distance when it came to everyday, normal social interactions. Talking to people at church, in the grocery mart, or at a coffee shop was difficult. Normally, being an introvert, it just compounded things when I had to stay away from even casual interaction. Spit and saliva could travel across the air through a sneeze or cough, especially when colds and sickness produce bad bacteria that get onto everything. Things as simple as a handshake were out of the question.

I had quite a lot of things to face in life. My health was lost. My educational career was shot. My family had no idea, nor understood how to accept or understand my daily living requirements and stipulations. Either most friends freaked out because they did not understand, saw their mortality, or refused to see me this way compared to how I was before I got sick.

I was in the middle of a whirlwind of survival. The only way to stay alive was to do my treatments and keep moving forward. I wanted to see my daughter grow up, develop into her dreams and potential, and see her married someday. This mindset helped me to stay focused on the task at hand, safe, and out of harm's way. It also made me very lonely and secluded, limited, and stinted in every single area of my life.

My life, or what was left of it, hinged on a machine for treatment, stabilization, and survival. It was carefully and methodically cleaning my blood, overseen by a team of kidney nurses and an in-house kidney doctor, or nephrologist. I also had a nutritionist who helped me avoid foods that may cause weight gain, but doing so was negligible because of my miraculous, unexplainable, frequent urination and lack of fluid retention.

Despite having favor from God in some areas, the first few months were very difficult in the chair, feeling sorry for myself and crying until I fell asleep during treatment. Rolling around in my pain and misery, I often complained about my limitations. No one at the dialysis unit blamed me, because we were all dealing with staying alive. It would have been acceptable to let my surroundings of all the people in the unit affect me, just going with the flow, allowing depression to take hold.

I was told by my nurses that this was a grieving time in my life, and I needed to slowly accept where I was in reality, letting myself adjust to dialysis life. But after some months had gone by, I had faced my situation of centering my life on a machine. I inevitably embraced my second home, the kidney dialysis unit.

It was a humbling, yet much-needed, grieving process in acknowledgement of my circumstances. I did not know what would happen to me from day to day, nor if I would ever stop getting dialysis treatments to keep me alive. But just sitting there getting my blood cleaned was not adequate for me.

Making a gradual, personal choice to persevere through the pain and discomfort was important to my well-being and helped set an example for others in the center. If I wanted to, I could have just refused treatment and gone home to die since dialysis was ultimately voluntary. I would slip into a confused and foggy state, my brain and body overcome with poisons. After a few weeks, slipping into a coma was a reality, then death. But what good would that have done for anybody? I never thought of giving up like this, but this option was always out there if I gave in to defeat and negativity.

It is a hard and brutal truth that some simply chose this route. I saw several stop trying to live, refusing treatment, eating a lot of food, or not showing up. Weekly death became a common reality in my world of kidney dialysis. To me, this would have been suicide because my soul was worth infinitely more than throwing the dice and taking chances with my eternal salvation. Putting my life in God's hands meant I did not sit around and live off a machine without taking further steps to enhance my chances at living a long and prosperous life; this included getting a kidney transplant. My nephrologist told me that my health status allowed me the opportunity to get tested to become a kidney recipient. If I qualified, my name would be put on a waiting list until a donor came along that most closely fit my blood and tissue type.

Excited about this possibility, Dad and I drove to the Iowa City, Iowa, Veterans Memorial Hospital, where I was put through many types of tests. I had an MRI brain scan, a chemical stress test, extensive blood work, and a four hundred and fifty question psychology test. Doctors, nurses, and surgeons talked to me at length about what being on a transplant list meant and what the surgery entailed. Psychologists and social workers spoke with me and asked questions about my emotional, social, and behavioral status. Post-transplant emotional and psychological ramifications of both the donor and the recipient were explained. I was also informed of social, emotional, and career implications.

I was questioned about my financial status, family connections, and if I had someone who could help me before, during, and after the transplant to get settled post-surgery. Social workers interviewed me about my overall situation and outlook in life. They wanted to get to know me, and through a series of steps, probed deep into my environmental status and perceptions. There was no end to the amount or variation of in-person or on-paper qualifications needed to become a potential kidney recipient.

I was thoroughly impressed that the veteran administration has this thorough a screening process. This method filtered who was best qualified and could handle the vastly intricate and important responsibility of receiving a million-dollar organ transplant. The process rivaled the strictest attention to detail I possessed during my service in the Navy.

The interviews, questionnaires, and all the rest took many days to complete. Once finished, my overall qualifications were sent to a transplant board for further review. They would be the final say-so. If they said no, I would be living on a machine for the rest of my life until Jesus healed me or took me home.

Thankfully, after many weeks of waiting, I was notified that I would be put on a waiting list to receive a kidney. I had been viewed as an outstanding candidate to receive a transplant by surgeons who reviewed my case, doctors who went over my charts, and others. My overall health, having no accompanying medical issues, or any record of drug use or anomalies in my tests, revealed a perfect transplant recipient qualification.

According to where you live, you are placed into a specific section of the country to receive a kidney, so my name was then entered into a database of my region. Even after all of this was complete, I still had slim chances of getting a transplant because of my O-negative blood type. I could give blood and be a potential organ donor to anyone, but I could not receive an organ or blood from anyone. However, this did not mean for me to have a fatalistic outlook, but I prayed and believed that I would receive a kidney, regardless of the odds. Acting on faith, I moved forward in Jesus and continued to do what I could to better my quality of life.

Chapter 29:

UNEXPLAINABLE SURGERY

My nephrologist, who came around every Wednesday and checked up on his patients, saw on my chart that I had had my temporary chest port for seven months. He suggested to me that it was time to start thinking about other means of kidney dialysis. Different types could provide me with varying levels and values of life, according to what I wanted to have installed.

Since I had no comorbidity, I had choices. Besides, having these two hoses taped onto the right of my chest had become more of a bother than an asset in my life. It was time for something different.

The peritoneal cavity dialysis system offered at home and in-center treatments was a system of blood cleansing requiring a curled-up hose burrowed into the hollow part of your body below the small intestine. Fluid would drain from a bag into the body through this pipe, soak up all the poison, and then be drained out. Nope, I did not like the idea of becoming a life-size beer keg.

The second kind of dialysis, and the one I opted for, was hemodialysis. It is offered at home and in-unit treatment. This kind would be performed by a fistula installed into a certain part of my body, accessed with needles.

I chose hemodialysis performed in my dialysis unit. I knew the nurses, the procedures, and my nephrologist was there, who did an excellent job of keeping tabs on his patients. I went to the Columbia, Missouri, veteran's hospital, and had preliminary vein mapping performed to see where the fistula would be created. Because the veins in my lower forearm were too small, it would be installed in my upper arm, between the bicep and the forearm. I returned for my fistula procedure a few weeks later, ready for this next phase.

I was taken back to Columbia by a friend who lived near me, and checked into surgery. Mapping of my veins again with ultrasound two weeks prior indicated that the ones in my lower forearms were still too small to access. They had to be a certain initial diameter for strength and gradual growth when tied to an artery between tendons and ligaments in my wrist, and be able to be accessed for kidney dialysis. The alternate plan was to go into my left bicep and tie the vein located in the interior bend of my arm to a major artery for ideal blood withdrawal and replacement.

I was wheeled back on a gurney to the cold surgery prep waiting area, and an IV was placed in the top of my right hand. A few minutes later, I was taken into the operating room. The anesthesiologist put the mask on my face, and the next thing I remember was waking up, lying in my hospital bed. Feeling something odd, I glanced down and saw that the skin on the side of my left lower wrist had been sewn together. That was weird, because before the operation, I was told that it was not a possibility.

The chief surgeon came in to explain what happened, or rather, what he could not explain. Everything was a go in the operating room, and his team was ready to open up a place in the upper bend of my arm. Just as they proceeded to do so, the surgeon stopped and told his team he was going to recheck my lower left forearm. When they opened up my wrist, something supernatural had happened. Between the time of the vein mapping, a few weeks before, and the surgery, the forearm vein that was too narrow to use had somehow grown four centimeters, enough to be used as my fistula access.

The surgeon had no reason or medical data to support this vein growth phenomenon, because it cannot happen. Surprised to say the least, he told his surgical team to reset and move forward with the forearm fistula access. They accessed the vein that ran along the side of my arm through the wrist and connected it to the radial artery below. Another cool thing was that I am right-handed. The fistula ended up in my left forearm, so I could eat, write, and perform everyday functions while protecting the access.

After surgery, I had someone drive me back home, and the next day to my dialysis unit. I still needed to use my chest catheter until the newly created dialysis site healed adequately over the next few months. I walked into my dialysis center and was greeted with warm welcomes because I was now part of the "inner circle" of hemodialysis patients.

According to the other patients in the unit, this marked an important rite of passage for kidney dialysis patients, the transition from emergency catheter to needle sticks. They joked about it, and I gave it right back to them. I could not fully appreciate their sense of humor until I started getting stuck. Their humor turned out to be very warped and pure evil.

After the wrist attachment point healed, it was time to start sticking my new access. The nurses did all of the usual prepping, cleaned out and around my chest access, set up my meds, took my blood pressure, performed fluid and weight level checks, and then it was time. Two needles with tubes attached to them and to the machine were produced. I had put some deadening cream on my forearm earlier that morning that was made to help lessen the pain of the procedure, considering the needle was as thick as a dime.

Nothing could have prepared me for my fellow dialysis buddies' demented humor wrapped in the rite of passage. The nurse took one of the one-inch in diameter, sixteen-gauge needles and told me to turn my head. The guys who were on their machines next to me just looked my way, smiling but not saying a word. A few more giggled and just stared as the torture began.

The nurse pushed the first needle into my vein until an audible pop could be felt, indicating he had penetrated the vein wall, then pulled it back out a little and straightened it parallel to my forearm. I grunted in severe agony, but not so much that my neighbors knew. I would not give them the pleasure of gloating, but I was pretty sure they saw my painfully twisted-up face.

She inserted the other one, then slid the needles all the way up inside the vein until the plastic neck, or top of the needle, met the opening to my arm. Both hoses were then taped down on my arm to prevent the needles from blowing back out due to the blood pressure of the radial artery flowing through the vein connection. Mission accomplished.

The initial cleaning process of the kidney dialysis machine was set to a low filtering speed, then turned up over time. The vein needed an adjustment period after getting poked so many times, and the pressure of the blood getting pulled and reinserted into my body. Scar tissue gradually built up around my fistula on each side of the forearm vein from the needle sticks, and the nerves slowly became less sensitive. Eventually, both needles were increased to fifteen gauge, larger than a pencil lead, but they took it like a man and stopped using the deadening cream.

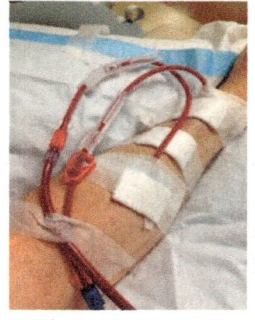

A healthy person's functioning set of kidneys constantly cleans all of the blood volume's impurities and toxins. Twenty-four hours a day, seven days a week, three hundred and sixty-five days a year, they help support the cardiovascular, skeletal, and endocrine systems. So, my body had all of these impurities building up in between visits, affecting all of them. According to the nurses and doctors, this left me minimally healthy and my body constantly trying to resist sickness, disease, bacteria, and a whole host of other medical issues that could kill me at any point. But I believed otherwise.

Because my body kept most of these poisons between treatments, it was beneficial and desirable that my fistula would grow sooner rather than later. When getting stuck, the repeated penetration and blood flow going in and out of my arm's vein resulted in responding like a muscle. Much like being a bodybuilder in my early years, my muscles grew the more I exercised them.

The more I worked out my muscles, the more they adjusted to the amount of weight I did and the frequency with which I used them. Similarly, the more I was poked in my vein access, the more it was worked out, and the larger the vein became. Over time, thick scar tissue developed on each side of the vein access from the pricks of the needles, appearing like white marks on my skin. Others who were going to poke needles into my arm would have an idea of what to do because they could see where I had been poked before, at least this is what I thought would happen.

Before I went on a trip out of town, I made sure there was access to a dialysis facility. The real trick was to find one that did the job right the first time. I called and set an appointment at a facility down where my brother lived. I drove into the parking lot, and did not have a good feeling the second I walked through the door.

First of all, I waited a while past my specified appointment time. Then, acting as if I were more of a hindrance than a patient, the nurse led me down a hall and took me to a chair in the back of the dialysis treatment facility. I sat in the chair next to people who had several types of long and swollen scars all over their arms.

One man had multiple bulges in his bicep and forearm, indicating that whoever was sticking him had repeatedly injured his veins, causing horrible results. This meant that he had serious trauma occurring when the needles were pushed through the side of the vein, causing blood to pool between the muscle and the skin. It was a blatant sign of negligence. This kind of medical abuse is excruciating, especially if it happens over and over, rendering the arm veins useless until they heal completely from the blowout. If not, other dialysis options would have to be explored.

The second the dialysis nurse started sticking me, I knew she was utterly and completely incompetent. She had not taken into consideration that my fistula was still only a few months old and had not been properly prepared for sticking. She proceeded without sterilizing my arm before the first needle, going through the vein across to the other side, where blood went into the muscle. Swelling of the area was immediate, the pain making me jump out of the chair.

Then this ridiculous nurse tried again but missed, causing blowouts above the place she started with, again without sterilizing my arm. She did not wait for the previous stick point to stop bleeding, and used no antiseptic or bandages on it. This torture went on for five more times, all of them missing the mark. Then, I lost it.

I told that incompetent piece of crap nurse in the best Navy rhetoric I could muster to stop sticking me. Standing up, I ordered her to put bandages on all of the bleeding holes and release me immediately. She proceeded to accuse me of moving my arm, not cooperating, and being unruly, resulting in repeated sticks.

I left that asinine excuse for a treatment facility and went back to my brother's house. I called the regional director's office of DaVita Dialysis later and complained about my treatment experience. To my knowledge, nothing was done to this person, and no repercussions

were experienced by that unit. But God saw.
These people were completely clueless. I was not just a patient; I was a person who had a say in who, what, when, where, and why I was getting any type of treatment. Any kind of trauma I experienced in my forearm fistula that day could have rendered it permanently useless. Not being able to access the vein would have caused me to have another emergency chest catheter inserted, starting the entire process of vein mapping all over again. Even with the best facility, it takes people who care to make kidney dialysis humane, even productive. However, some things cannot be controlled by dialysis nurses, especially when patients encounter unforeseen circumstances.

Modern developments in electronics, cleaning machinery, and refining the fluid removal process have led to vast developments in kidney dialysis equipment, but seeing people dying was still a reality. Patients died and were never seen again, often without warning. There was little to no time to say goodbye or get emotionally prepared for the loss of those I had just talked to the day before, or had become friends with. Whether by choosing dialysis treatment voluntarily or involuntarily, a patient's death often came in my hemodialysis world.

Any day of the week, someone in the unit could have a major health problem in the center. If a patient's blood pressure dropped or spiked during treatment to the point of cardiac arrest or fainting, an ambulance was called. The dialysis patient was loaded up onto a gurney and whisked away, often never to be seen again. On the other hand, some convinced themselves that dialysis was no longer an option and simply stayed home to pass away.

Patients deciding to eat and drink in excess or who

consumed fast food were rejecting the doctor's dietary requirements. This often resulted in too much weight gain between treatments and was extremely difficult to remove during treatments the very next day. Blatantly ignoring their body's needs usually caused negative reactions that resulted in coma, respiratory distress, heart attacks, and other health ailments.

Every Wednesday after treatment, I did cheat and went to my favorite donut shop to buy a few of my favorite sugar-laden, doughy, delicious pastries; donut holes and an apple fritter. Besides occasional sherbet, these were the only times I ate. My blood sugar levels always hovered around 72 mg/dl, much lower than the average of 70-90 mg/dl. My doctor said it was amazing. Praise God.

Most, if not all, patients during my time slot for dialysis refused to take their situation in life seriously, not being proactive in taking care of their health. Ranging from twenty-somethings to those in their eighties, patients seemed to ignore relevant limits on dialysis, including what kinds of food to eat and how much. The obvious neglect is reflected in tremendous weight gain, apparent acting-out issues, and even disregard for interaction with their doctor, nurses, and fellow patients. I often thought about these people I grew to call my friends, and it bothered me, causing personal anxiety and worry.

Watching my television one early morning during treatment, feelings of being utterly helpless to others' misgivings about their health hit me all at once. So, I stopped trying to change what was going on with other patients. I was fighting for them, hoping they would see my sincerity and need for them to stay alive, but doing it for them would never be enough. They had to ultimately make their own decisions. As much as losing friends due to self-neglect hurt, it was ultimately their choice to live or die.

From then on, I would not let people's treatment of themselves bring me down, no matter how tough it became. I would focus on what I could do in my predicament, finding strength from God. I had done this in past academic, social, and military situations, drawing from these lessons in this fight to live. To help myself embrace this part of dialysis positively, I started simply celebrating life with others in the unit who wanted to persevere no matter what, praying for those who did not.

John, an old cowboy with a thick Arkansas accent, loved his beer. He was a good old Baptist cowboy who always had a smile on his face, and I instantly liked the guy. Everyone who met him did, too.

John joked about life and told us about times of drinking at his favorite bar or working in the garden. He shared how his wife often yelled at him for drinking. For John, drinking was the last thing in life that made him happy, and he got a kick out of making his wife upset, but loved her very much. I always had a feeling that his weekend drinking binges would get the better of him, and sure enough, I came into the unit for dialysis one morning and asked where he was. The nurse said he had died the day before.

Mary was a small, elderly woman who always walked into the unit very, very quietly. After weighing in, she shuffled slowly across the floor in her little slippers and stood by her chair very patiently. It was always evident that she had gained a lot of fluid between dialysis sessions because her breathing was labored and she looked bloated, no matter how much dialysis she did. It never helps that she rarely finishes her sessions.

Mary used an oxygen bottle to breathe during and after treatment, and reminded me of my great-grandmother being soft spoken with a quiet demeanor. I tried to engage her as much as possible when she was awake. Mary often appeared to be incoherent and indifferent to those around her, passing out more than once. She died within a month of John.

Matt and Janice were a married couple doing kidney dialysis on different shifts. The center did this to help married patients stay focused on treatment. They suffered with heart issues, voluntary resistance to treatment, and, from what I sensed, an overall depression. I was never able to talk to Janice, but an occasional talk with Matt revealed a very cool hippie guy of the 1960s, stuck in the present day.

Matt, the "free energy hippie" as he was known to me, loved his Ford hybrid car. He always kept things pretty low-key and easy-going, and from what I could gather, was someone of means. He had a way of taking others out of a negative mindset, even though he always seemed to also be pretty mundane. It was an odd character mix, but where our lives were in the unit, nothing was out of question. His wife died first, and shortly thereafter, with what I surmised was a case of giving up one's will, Matt died shortly after her at home.

Someone who may still be alive today out of sheer bull-headedness and who always kept the place jumping was an old Irishman named Larry. He had a rough go of it before arriving in dialysis after I did, and had lost a leg due to cancer. In spite of his struggles, he was the neighborhood storyteller and always appreciated a good cut-down, as long as you could take what you gave.

It often became a competition between me and Larry about who could put down the other one the worst. This friendly banter always resulted in roars of laughter from patients and nurses alike. I looked forward to seeing that crazy dude every time I went to dialysis. To his credit, Larry did get one over on me more than once and became an integral part of my dialysis family. And as if he were any cooler, he drove a very fast convertible he worshipped, and everyone talked about it.

Belle always had a smile on her face and always spoke of God. Eating those forbidden hamburgers and fries while being dialyzed, she beamed with God's presence. Knowing she was ruining her health was constantly on my mind, but Belles's grin was infectious and distracted me from seeing the hurt she was doing to herself. Belle and I prayed a few times together. She was very concerned about her health, but not enough to cut out the junk food. One morning, she passed out again, and an ambulance was called. She died a short time later.

Chapter 30:

DIALYSIS REALITY

Having friends in the dialysis unit was bittersweet. I was doing my part to help them overcome their difficult situations, often to no avail. Frustrating as it was, my heart was to help others defy their lies, starting where I was. Since I had prior teaching and counseling experience, I decided to start substitute teaching a few days a week on the days I did not get dialyzed and working out in the evenings. I started to gain favor with a few teachers, asking me to help with their students when they needed a substitute. Since I could only teach a few days a week, I did what I could. Working with students of all ages deepened my level of empathy for behaviorally challenged, autistic, those with special needs, and students who were in wheelchairs. I began to see past the superficial actions of these kids, looking deeper into their hearts and minds.

I was able to feel their hurts and listen to what they were saying through their verbalized thoughts and actions. God showed me during this time that my life of suffering through rejection, misunderstanding, labeling, and judgment had purpose. He was developing in me a deeper understanding of what students and people in general were going through. This process activated a level of discernment I had not had before relating to them to a degree never before realized. It was as if I could see right into their hearts and minds.

Having friends in the dialysis unit was bittersweet. I was doing my part to help them overcome their difficult situations, often to no avail. Frustrating as it was, my heart was to help others defy their lies, starting where I was. Since I had prior teaching and counseling experience, I decided to start substitute teaching a few days a week on the days I did not get dialyzed and working out in the evenings.

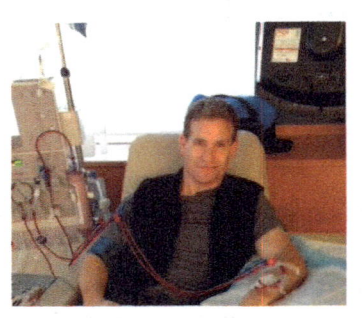

I started to gain favor with a few teachers, asking me to help with their students when they needed a substitute. Since I could only teach a few days a week, I did what I could. Working with students of all ages deepened my level of empathy for behaviorally challenged, autistic, those with special needs, and students who were in wheelchairs. I began to see past the superficial actions of these kids, looking deeper into their hearts and minds.

I was able to feel their hurts and listen to what they were saying through their verbalized thoughts and actions. God showed me during this time that my life of suffering through rejection, misunderstanding, labeling, and judgment had purpose.

He was developing in me a deeper understanding of what students and people in general were going through. This process activated a level of discernment I had not had before relating to them to a degree never before realized. This heightened sense of awareness revolutionized my outlook and understanding of all I encountered, extending beyond my book smarts and mindset of curriculum, policy, and educational tactics. I had been teaching for a little while and started to feel pretty good about life in general, and followed the urge to expand my life opportunities even further.

After nine months of initial dialysis adjustment, I had the desire to start dating. I was initially pretty self-conscious about meeting women because of my forearm fistula scars and bandages. But once I realized there was nothing that could be done about it, the alternative of loneliness was not an option for me. I decided to jump into dating with both feet, scars and all. All they could do was say no.

I found an online dating site and looked through hundreds of profiles to find a woman remotely interesting. Most turned out to be illegitimate, had fake profiles, or were not interesting in the least. After spending a few weeks on it, I decided to change my plan of attack and began dating the old-fashioned way.

I had started substitute teaching for a few weeks when I met another pretty substitute teacher and asked her to meet me at a yogurt shop. Yeah, kind of cheesy, but it was a public place with people, a comfortable setting, and plenty of light to keep it objective with no pressure. We talked for a little while, joked around a bit, and had a pretty good time. Conversation seemed to go smoothly, and things were looking good until I told her that I was a dialysis patient.

I mentioned in passing about needles in my arm, her eyes widened, taking on a defensive posture. Then, turning a slight shade of white, she proceeded to tell me that needles and blood horrified her. It was not like I gave her graphic details about what I endured, just briefly shared about different parts of my life, including my dialysis.

My treatment was a large part of my life, and anyone I dated would need to know. I figured I had better tell her up front to see how she handled it. Far better to tell someone before emotions were set and a relationship was established. Realizing she was quickly losing interest, we talked for only a few more minutes, and I cut it short.

After we went our separate ways, I called her up that evening and told her I noticed she was pretty uncomfortable, and not everyone can handle my condition or station in life. Inside, I felt rejected and left out because dialysis was now my dating nemesis, but I wished her well and hung up. I decided to face the fact that even though I understood what it was like from my point of view, potential dates may not simply accept me for me. Instead of convincing her and sensing how it would sooner or later inevitably turn out, I faced my situation and embraced my dating predicament.

Trying to develop any kind of significant relationship seemed impossible, and as much as I tried to help people feel at ease and not get freaked out, it did not work. I just could not hide what I was going through with my health, or make anyone understand what I was dealing with physically. Dating became harder and harder to validate, becoming more of a fleeting idea in my mind. People, from close friends to family, quickly disappeared or simply stopped contacting me when they found out I was on kidney dialysis.

The general attitude of others was one of not knowing what the hell I was going through. The women I met were initially attracted to me, but then nothing happened. These women were living in an alternate reality, one in which I could no longer dwell.

For that matter, I could have said screw it, gone crazy, and slept with every woman that came my way, but that would not have honored God. Instead, I temporarily shut down all forms of dating but still had to do something to help me feel like I was living and not just surviving. Sitting in my treatment chair one morning, watching television with the cushion warmer turned up, I had this thought of when I used to enjoy working out.

My nephrologist came into the dialysis center a few days a week to monitor his patients, check on their well-being, and measure data. On Wednesdays, he came into the center to talk to me on my Monday, Wednesday, and Friday treatment days. He was a cool doctor and was actually the one who first saw me when I moved to Missouri, way before my kidneys shut down. It seemed that this was put into motion to remind me that God is in control, seeing everything past, present, and future.

On one of his visitation days, I asked my Doctor what he thought of exercising. He said research suggested that it helped lower the severity of side effects, with fluid retention kept at bay in some patients. He was already impressed at how well my health had been maintained, and for reasons unexplainable, how I was losing weight between dialysis sessions. So he thought I could really benefit from moderately pursuing it. Doc also said research suggested some form of exercise helped dialysis patients with emotional stability.

I took this as a personal challenge. I was not going to settle for doing the minimum or a little exercise. No matter what, it would be all or nothing, and if dying was the result, so be it. I knew where I was going, and my mind was already there. I feel the need to say at this point that I understand the word "die" has been mentioned more often than one would normally encounter. In my life, this term was a big part of my everyday existence, and I had to face the fact that I could have left this Earth at any point.

I saw friends die regularly, having about ten do so within one year. And I would do anything and everything to blatantly ignore negativity, fighting to overcome despite the obvious. My life is still lived with the same zeal and fervor, setting an example for myself and others with whom I come in contact.

After looking around at a few local gyms, I signed up at one where there was a large indoor track. I had to be careful not to join outside gyms to have excessive sun exposure during exercise. I was extremely susceptible to skin cancer due to immune compromise from dialysis, so when I found out the gym had an indoor running area, that was perfect. It ran outside the entire perimeter of the gym.

Indoor bike riding, weightlifting, cross-training, and

all kinds of other exercises were available. The energy of the people and athletes working out in that gym was infectious. According to the large signs posted along the walls lining the track, it took seven and a half laps to run a mile. I decided to count laps rather than miles.

I was psyched to be working out again, loving the feeling, energy, stress relief, and accomplishment it provided. It was the ideal escape from living off a machine, finally feeling a part of making my life better. Every day, I looked forward to crushing any personal psychological, mental, or physical limits.

I made up my mind that no matter how painful or draining my dialysis sessions were, how badly my brain was pounding with painful fire, or how tired I was, I would make myself go to the gym immediately after treatment. Hitting the track would be my first exercise, warming up and stretching, before getting into the lane. I started slowly, walking and running every other lap.

To prevent injuring myself, I slowly built up the strength in my bones, ligaments, muscles, cardiovascular system, and heart, adapting to exercise again. I had not run in years, so progressive improvement was the name of the game. However, I did not care what my body was telling me. Discomfort, soreness, foot bruises, or any other kind of brain fog, extreme headaches, arm pain, lethargy, or any other dialysis effects would not stop my progress. I was completely determined to overcome any deterrent, fully focused on the task.

I knew God was giving me the ability to exercise as I stepped out in faith, defying the lies of those who told me I should not exercise at all. It did not help that doubt and unbelief came from friends worried about my health, telling me to use my "common sense" when it came to my dialysis and self-care. These seemingly sincere remarks were meant to help, but were disguised as limitations. When I slowly but steadily kept at it, I built up to working out every day of the week.

I literally stepped out in stubborn, determined faith on that track to face and embrace my limits, then surpass them as God met me there. Soon, I began to see real progress.

Within a few months, running and walking turned into three miles steadily running, and over the next several months, I built up to nine and a half miles running continuously. Often, I saw people walking slowly or not really giving it their all. I would run past them in their lane, give them a big smile, and enthusiastically tell them that they could do more. I would share about being a kidney dialysis patient, and if I could run around the track with everything I was dealing with, they could push themselves a little bit further. I loved the smiles from them as they tried.

When I reached a good running pace and mileage, I introduced swimming. This exercise had always been one of my favorite exercises, going back to my Navy days, second to weightlifting, and it felt really good to get back into the water after several years. I started out with an hour of swimming after running and then worked up to three hours of laps at a time. I never counted the distance.

I used the Olympic-sized pool, and a true lap was swimming to one end and back, where I started. I became so good at long swims that I was invited to train with the triathlon team in town. That was an incredible experience, and although not as fast as the other swimmers were, I loved the interaction and connections made while training with the team.

I also reached a point of being able to ride my bike thirty-five miles. Sometimes I combined two of the three exercises on the same day, pushing myself beyond my limits, my body, and beyond the impossible. I would turn up the intensity when I felt like I was starting to settle, then push it even farther.

With all of this working out, I went down to one hundred and seventy-eight pounds, maintaining a very low body fat percentage. My endurance levels were very high, and my blood pressure was great, with a resting heart rate of fifty-two beats per minute. I still never retained any fluid between treatments, and my blood test levels were always perfect.

I developed mental and physical fortitude while stepping out in faith to face my limits and embrace the possibilities of surpassing my physical abilities. What resulted was the recreation of my potential for accomplishments through faith in Jesus Christ. If I needed to take a rare nap after treatment, I did. As soon as my eyes opened, I quickly headed to the gym, pushing through the laziness.

My zeal became contagious, rubbing off on others everywhere I went. What I was doing provided an opportunity to motivate. Whether on purpose or by accident, others were uplifted and blessed, and seeing people succeed was my greatest reward.

Chapter 31:

DOCTORATE COMEBACK

One afternoon, I was driving back from the veteran's clinic for some blood tests, and suddenly had several thoughts flood my mind. What if I were to go back to school now? Was this a good time? Can I handle the school load, dialysis, working out, maybe dating, and all the rest? Is this God's plan for my life?

Sandwiched in between these questions, hiding until just the right time to affect my mind like a deceitful snake was doubt. I began to feel it creep in as I took steps to find out more about the logistics and procedures of starting back on my doctorate. It had been almost a year and a half since I stopped school. As much as I wanted to become a doctor, I was in a very different place in my life at this time. I had become completely content with never returning to school and never thought about it, until now.

Over the next few days, I prayed and sought God to

take away the desire. No matter how much I tried to ignore the idea of returning to school, it never left. It was as if my destiny of becoming a doctor was set in stone by God, and nothing would stop me from earning it, not even me.

I called up the Lindenwood doctoral office after dialysis treatment to set an appointment with the Director of the Southwest Missouri Extension Campus of Lindenwood University. He was the director of the program when I first started and still served in this role. He was also the doctor who said it was fine that I needed to stop my pursuit when I started dialysis, and was always open to me restarting it once I was in a healthy place physically.

I woke up the next morning and felt an overall peace about everything. This was confirmation because I really wanted to move forward in this endeavor. I had a renewed strength in my academics, looking forward to talking with Dr. Tim about it all.

I drove over to his office, thinking about how to greet him and what to say. Walking through the front door, I met his secretary, said who I was, and to my surprise, she called out to Dr. Tim in a laid-back manner. I had known him to be pretty easy-going despite his academic status, but the way I was announced seemed to be not only relaxed but also very engaging and welcoming.

I walked into his office and was greeted with a hearty handshake as we sat down. He asked me how I had been and what I had been up to the last year and a half. I told him all about my dialysis sessions, how God helped me through difficulties, and that everything in my life was going very well. At the time, I did not know he was a Christian, but when I mentioned that God was in control no matter what, he seemed pleased with my answer. I also told him I was staying fit.

I could tell he was searching out my overall state of mind and health about returning to the doctoral program. I volunteered the overall status of my life, such as working out and dialysis, to reassure him of my abilities as a doctoral student after everything I had been through. Without saying a word, he produced a document and placed it between us on the desktop. On this yellow piece of paper were classes of the entire program, the ones I had already taken, and others I had to take. This was the sign of approval I was looking for, validating my acceptance of Dr. Tim to get back to studying.

We went over which classes I had already taken in 2013, the ones I still needed to complete, in addition to any that I had taken in my graduate degree program in school counseling that might transfer. There were a couple of classes I was able to bypass because some graduate schooling counted as doctoral credits. This would help me finish quicker and keep me on the three-year mark for total time spent on doctorate completion.

Wanting to pursue my degree amid everything else in my life, I was somehow balancing, which seemed to give me favor in Dr. Tim's eyes and created a strong bridge to help me get plugged back into my doctoral pursuit. The program I was pursuing was an accelerated course of study, going to school year-round, condensing the seven-year average time of doctorate pursuit into three. He was convinced, as I already was, that I could do it successfully. After settling my course schedule and working out all of the parts of my doctorate track with him for the upcoming semester, I signed and dated the official document. This single act allowed me back into the accelerated Doctoral program at Lindenwood University, followed by Dr. Tim doing the same.

He turned to me after signing and gave me great inspiration, telling me that he was very impressed with my tenacity, perseverance, and steadfast ability to push through inevitable odds to get back to school. He believed that, despite everything I was going through, he felt I had proved myself well enough to attack the rest of my program with diligence and thoroughness. I was very humbled to hear this and told him that I would not let him or the program down. I had been given a second chance by him, the doctoral department, and most importantly by God. I would not squander it.

With a huge sigh of relief, we shook hands. After agreeing on when I would start back, I walked out of Dr. Tim's office with heightened confidence. It felt like a giant, indescribable weight of delayed gratification being lifted off my shoulders.

Now adding school to the mix, my crazy existence was about to get even crazier, and I welcomed it with open arms. The first thing to do was to develop a schedule to balance everything. Since the classroom curriculum began at the 7000 level (a bachelor's degree at 100), I needed to prioritize studying and project completion.

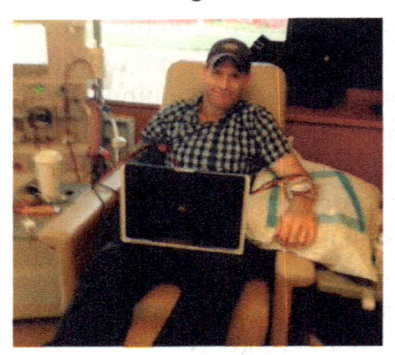

I needed to set aside time to research several hundred different kinds of resources in my dissertation from all over the world. These peer-reviewed doctoral papers, published journal articles from doctoral-level literature, previously proven research, and other types of resources too numerous to mention here, had to be within the last five years of my projected doctoral defense. I was required to discover a novel concept, gap, or idea no one had ever considered in the field of Education, internationally. I also had to develop an entirely new way to measure my proposed discovery for research, developing interviews and measuring instruments, questionnaires, and others. All of this was just the tip of the iceberg.

If I ran late in getting my doctorate finished, I was required to find additional resources, delaying me even further. Furthermore, every single sentence in my almost 200-page dissertation required a reference at the end of it, stating the author(s) and date of publication. To overcome these and other strenuous coursework requirements, staying on task to complete my doctorate in three years, I brought my laptop to dialysis.

The first time my nurses saw me typing, they asked what was up. I just told them I was working on my doctorate. They smiled and congratulated me, being some of my biggest supporters.

The pain and fatigue from dialysis I often experienced during my doctorate pursuit were of no matter to me. I believed and stepped out in faith, like many times before, knowing that I would and could overcome this challenge if I faced it and embraced every aspect. Denying it would have done nothing but placed doubt and second-guessing my abilities, given by God. Jesus infused me with the supernatural power to pursue it, and I did with every ounce of energy possible.

I attacked my academics with a raw tenacity not seen

since military training. Collaborating with my new doctoral cohort went pretty well, and I made some pretty good friends who shared the same kind of Type A personality. Together, we worked our butts off, cheering each other on. We were in it, all or nothing.

Dr. Eric Shannon Parr

Chapter 32:

GIFT OF LIFE

The next year and a half after starting back to school was a blur. Between researching and discovering the gap between facility management mandates versus student requirements of training and learning environments, and thrice weekly kidney treatments, my life was insane. I lightened up on training for a triathlon but still stayed in shape. After another year of eighteen-hour research days, the light at the end of the tunnel of school completion was beginning to emerge out of the dark, temporary insanity of my doctoral pursuit. Through it all, the favor of the Lord was with me until crossing the finish line.

My life was busy for sure, and things were looking great except for mom's simultaneous battle with pancreatic cancer over the last few years. She also fell and broke her hip, requiring two hip replacements because the first one caused a horrible bacterial infection.

She was very contagious to a person like me who was immunosuppressed, keeping me from seeing her for the last part of her life. If I had come close to her, I could have died.

I was viewed by some people who I thought had my back as not caring about my mom's situation. But you know, when it came down to it, my health, my doctoral pursuits, and my overall quality of life had to be balanced. Believe me, my heart was with my mother through every cancerous battle she fought.

While hanging out with dad on my last visit with mom, she asked to see only me in her room. As I walked in, a quiet urgency filled the air, so I closed the door and sat on the bed at her side. I looked at mom's little brown eyes, held her hand, and smiled my best sorrowful smile. She asked me, "Is it okay if I go home (to Heaven) now?"

I replied, "Yes, Mom, you can go." She then said, "I want to make sure you are going to be okay." I said, "Everything will be okay." "Okay," she said, closing her eyes. I fell silent and hugged her extremely emaciated body that was all of seventy-five pounds, and walked out of the room.

A few weeks later, with my brother at her side, she took her last breath on Earth and went to be with Jesus. She would no longer have to take care of her family, put herself second, or sacrifice her health, well-being, and personal desires. Mom did her part, showing others the epitome of how to fight through hurt and overcome impossibilities. She is the strongest person I have ever known. I know I will see her again, and although she did not get to see me become a doctor, I know she would have been very proud.

As much as mom's death was a horrible thing,

February 27, 2017, brought news of life. I was at home doing research when my girlfriend received a phone call from one of her friends she met through a work function. She told her that something horrible had just happened to her son a few hours ago, and she needed to know if I still needed a kidney donor.

Writing this sentence, I still cannot begin to comprehend what she did. This lady lost her fifteen-year-old son and was still in shock. She was trying to get things situated with all of the medical issues, family, and all the rest, yet had the capacity to call and be concerned about someone else she had not even met. And miraculously, my girlfriend had only just met this colleague a month prior to all of this happening.

This amazing mother said she would check with the hospital to see if her son would be a good match for me to receive one of his kidneys. Monitoring the status of her son's body that was on life support at that point was of utmost importance because his tissue type had to match mine almost perfectly. It turns out her son was a selfless, amazing young man who had decided years before to be an organ donor. Together with his parents, they signed himself up to give his organs to others, helping them survive and live on after him if such a day ever came.

This grieving mother, whose son just died, thought of nothing else but my well-being. She told us over the next few hours, through phone calls, the status of tissue and other types of testing, keeping us in the loop of what the doctors were thinking and doing. Soon, my transplant coordinator called me and gave us the rundown of what they were looking at as far as traveling to the Iowa City, Iowa, Veteran Memorial Hospital.

My kidney transplant team in Iowa was notified that a

possible match was located in Missouri, and tests were being performed for confirmation. I was called and told to get packed and ready to go just in case everything lined up. A few hours later, tissue type confirmation tests were still being run. My transplant coordinator, in agreement with the surgeons, told me to get on the road because things were looking good overall. We all agreed it was better to start our trip rather than have the surgical team wait until we arrived.

Without hesitation, we packed up, jumped into the car, and headed north. The further we drove, the more the weather started to change and get colder, with snow now starting to fall. It was a beautiful and anxious scene mixed with anticipation, prayer, and falling snowflakes. These external weather changes somehow mimicked internal, physical changes that were about to happen. The life I knew was going to be transformed into a fresh, white, and new future.

Halfway through the trip, I received the call saying he and I were a perfect match for receiving the kidney. Not only that, but it was a near-perfect tissue match, something my surgeons and doctors had never seen before. Not only did I have the ideal organ transplant donor, but the donated kidney was exceedingly above anything I could have imagined, beyond even the top nephrologist's expectations. To God be praised.

When we arrived at the hospital, I was greeted with a rush of happy nurses and doctors who were ready to get the show on the road. I was directed to my room, settled in, and had some IVs put in my arms and hands for fluid and medications before, during, and after the procedure. My girlfriend was given directions from the hospital to the hotel where we would be staying for a month of post-transplant recuperation.

That evening of February 27, 2017, marked the last time I would have kidney dialysis. The doctors needed to make sure my blood was as filtered as possible before the transplant procedure, so I went to the dialysis unit upstairs to get my blood cleaned. During treatment, I quietly told the dialysis technician I was about to have kidney transplant surgery, and that I had been on dialysis for the last three years, and I was thankful it was over.

A few dialysis patients looked over and congratulated me. That eased my mind because statistically speaking, some people there did not have any kind of chance for a transplant, never living a life apart from a dialysis center. However, it turned out to be a group celebration that encouraged me.

That evening, I took my last medications and pre-surgical sterilizing shower, waiting with nervous excitement until it was time. One of many things the Veterans Administration does perfectly is to make sure its transplant patients are well taken care of and thoroughly informed. I was notified practically every half hour of the progress when my kidney would arrive in Iowa City, how the last-minute tests were going, and the projected surgery time.

A large group of people came into my room. This was my transplant team, consisting of surgeons, interns, nurses, physician assistants, nephrologists, anesthetists, surgical and nurse technicians, and many more. They went through the procedures with me, asked me how I was doing, and we hung out together a bit. It was amazing to know my team cared enough about not only the procedure but the person getting the transplant, an indelible mark in my mind I will have forever.

They notified us that the surgery was projected to last up to six hours. The donor kidney would be brought in, checked over again visually for any anomalies and defects, irrigated with saline, prepared, tested again for tissue matching, and then inserted into the peritoneal cavity below my stomach. After the procedure, I would be sent to the intensive care unit for a few hours or days for post-surgical procedures and observations, ensuring my new kidney was functioning properly, and then to my room.

As the evening went by, we continued to get updates in the room until the last call let us know everything was a go. The donor kidney was stable, and the team was awaiting my arrival in the surgical theater. Time was of the essence at this point because the longer a kidney stays outside of the body, the greater the chance of it contracting bacteria, disease, or a host of other issues. Additionally, any muddled alteration to its tissue type rendered it useless to me.

A few minutes before ten p.m. I was whisked away to begin my transplant surgery procedure. A few nurses followed close by, making sure I was still doing well, and asked me how I felt. I yelled down the hall from my rolling bed entourage, "Let's get this show on the road!" Laughter busted out down the hall, with me laughing the loudest. I was getting my kidney!

I went down a long highway and glanced through large windows, noticing doctors scrubbing up for surgery. We turned in that direction and entered the surgical auditorium. There was my life-giving team ready to perform the transplant.

A doctor welcomed me into what appeared to be something out of a science fiction movie with large monitors, machines, computers, and stainless steel instruments everywhere. Large theater lighting lit up the entire area, and at one end of the room were surgical bowls, with one that I could only guess held my gift of life.

I lay down on the cold and steel operating table with a cushion, and nurses put a thick, blue blanket on me for warmth until the procedure began. A nurse with smiling eyes gently asked me if I was ready. I nodded, and before I could breathe in twice, everything went black.

The next thing I remembered, I opened my eyes to a familiar scene, being back in the room with my girlfriend and nurses all around my bed. A severe, throbbing pain radiated from my lower stomach area, making my whole body hurt. I could barely move, much less turn or sit up on my power.

The entire right side of my body felt like it was sewn completely together in the middle. Any little turn or the slightest bend at the waist was impossible, pulling at reattached tissue and muscles. I was given pain medication via a hand-held trigger to self-administer when the agony hit me in waves, but it did not do a whole lot of good. However, considering the alternative of dying, I would have gladly endured all of this again.

A tube was inserted into my lower right side during surgery. This was used to drain out any residual fluid from the kidney attachment site, flowing into a small plastic bag, clipped to the bed. Other needles with tubes had been inserted into my arm on top of whatever I already had before surgery. These white sticky pads with leads were stuck on my chest, hooked up to machines and monitors hung on a stainless-steel looking metal tree. These helped nurses and doctors monitor my vitals, levels of oxygen, blood contents, administer medications, read blood pressure, and heart rate.

Swathed in yellow surgical iodine was where the miracle surgery took place. There was a swollen, red, and pink nine-inch scar resembling a hockey stick to the right of my belly button, extending from waist level to my lower pubic area. A catheter had been inserted during the transplant, catching any urine until my kidney and bladder were healed at the attachment points of the ureter. The head surgeon and some of the surgical staff entered my room to tell me how the procedure went.

After setting anesthesia levels, I was given five hundred milligrams of prednisone, which crushed my immune system, basically stopping it altogether. I was now completely susceptible to anything and everything under the sun. If a nurse happened to have even a cold, that could have been extremely deadly.

As the team prepared the donor kidney, the surgical team was aware of every single step they performed. Any slacking in sterilization, irrigation, or techniques instigated with the organ or my body during any part of the transplant procedure, and immediate infection and rejection of the organ was a huge probability. If the transplant process was deemed ineffective, closing me back up and putting me back on dialysis until a new kidney could be found would be the result.

Part of the surgical team prepped the site, opened me up, and tied things off while the other surgeons and surgical nurses kept the new donor kidney bathed and prepped in a saline solution until my body was ready to receive it. Once every part of the surgical team was set, they installed it, tying up blood vessels and arteries carrying blood flow to and from the new organ. Then the ureter was cut from the old kidneys, the area sutured, and then rerouted and sewn to the new organ. An eight-inch, flexible wire stent was inserted into the length of the ureter and sewn onto it at both ends. This wire brace helped to keep the sutured ureter in place until the attachment points were fully healed.

The incision and placement of my new kidney went very well. According to the surgeon, I was in such great shape that my strong stomach muscle tissue needed to be maneuvered in such a way to accommodate the new kidney, even though it was smaller than my original one. Miraculously, it only took twenty-five minutes for the transplanted kidney to start producing urine once connected. Normally, it takes a lot longer due to organs and tissues freezing up when they are touched during surgery. This is a self-preservation phenomenon of our bodies to protect organs from damage.

The transplant results, even though initially very positive, could have turned for the worse due to a hidden infection. The resulting inflamed areas around, above, and below the kidney might have hindered healing of the surgical site, resulting in the need to return to the hospital for fluid drainage. Then, a machine hooked up to my side with a tube stuck into where the kidney was would continuously suck out infected pus. I saw this happen to other patients as I was recuperating, and they were in torture.

My overall surgery was also much faster than expected, only taking three and a half hours from the time I was placed under anesthesia in the surgical theatre to the time I arrived back in my room. The lead surgeon of the transplant team said it could have taken six hours. Also, the usual follow-up day or two post-surgery in the

Intensive Care Unit was not needed. My body accepted the new organ exceptionally well. Thank you, Jesus.

When I woke up in the room, despite the pain and being out of it due to the anesthesia, there was an inner surge of strength I had never remembered having, even when I was healthy. It made me wonder just how long I was actually sick before this whole ordeal. Nevertheless, it was about moving forward.

My continuous lethargy was completely gone. I was no longer freezing to death, the insane itching ceased, and all of my joint pain vanished. When I first awoke in my room, the nurse said the color of my face had improved, having gone from a pale greenish-grey to a healthy, normal pink glow.

It is amazing what clean blood can do for you, especially when a kidney works. I went from only 10 % of my blood being purified in a dialysis session to 100%, twenty-four hours a day. My thinking, talking, and mental processing, even physical strength levels, were significantly better in spite of being very weak.

I was also notified of a tendency for scar tissue to build up around internal sutures, so the nurses helped me sit up on one side of my bed only a few hours after surgery. I did this as long as I could, starting with twenty minutes at a time. The next day, I was made to sit in a chair until the pain was unbearable. This necessary routine was to help strengthen the stomach muscles and layers of tissue surrounding them that were cut during the transplant procedure.

Sitting up under my strength for the first several hours over the next few days of recuperation was mind-bending, but I pushed through it. The next full day post-surgery, I started to walk up and down the halls with my girlfriend's assistance. The steroids and pain medication pumping through my veins helped very little, as I felt everything inside my lower gut pull and pinch like stabbing knives.

My girlfriend helped me stay upright as much as I could because I was completely out of it, doing things with my catheter that to this day I cannot remember. She said I flashed all of the staff with a stupid grin on my face as everyone looked at me. More than once, I stopped in the middle of the hallway, looked down at my catheter, and said, "Ok, it's ok!"

Over the next several days, the hundreds of milligrams of steroids, medications, pain meds, and anti-rejection drugs coursing through my body were progressively lowered until they met an acceptable level. I was freaking happy about that because I was flying higher than the clouds, not sleeping much at all, and had ridiculously horrific reactions to them. Each morning for the first three days, my muscles started quaking like I was having a gigantic seizure. My body stiffened up, causing horrible pain at the incision site, while shoving me into confusion and fear.

I hit the nurses' station button every time the muscle spasms happened, and they came running into the room to help me stand up. This was the only way to get them to lessen in intensity and frequency. It often took three nurses to help me upright.

Sometimes when I thought they took too long to come to my room, I forced through the extreme pain of pulling on the scar tissue and tried to stand up, crying from the agony I experienced. Hearing me scream from down the hall, they ran into my room, grabbed each side of me, and lifted me the rest of the way. I also stiffened up like a board, being "pharmaceutically electrocuted" with a million watts.

Every time this happened, the tremors and muscle quakes were torture. When a person has hundreds of milligrams of steroids surging through their body, it is ridiculous how the body seems to act. I was jacked up.

Standing eased the tremors a little and eventually subsided after four days. I was told later these were side effects and normal for transplant patients due to the ton of medications administered before, during, and after surgery. God, that was awful.

I walked three times a day up and down the hospital hallway in front of my room, holding onto the circular bar connected to the side of my medication tree. I called it my metallic tree of life that hung the monitors for blood pressure, oxygen sensor, medication level indicator, emergency nurse button, saline bags, and everything else in between. It was ridiculous how much stuff was hanging off that seemingly fragile stainless-steel pole. Nevertheless, I managed to keep it upright no matter how many times I tried to accidentally flip it over.

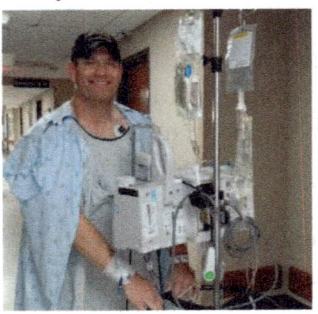

My girlfriend helped me tremendously with whatever I needed, getting information from the staff, doctors, and nurses, and helped me walk in a straight line up and down the hall. Because I was so out of it, she also kept me from acting like a goofball, stopping and talking to everyone I saw, slurring most of my words. I also heard from doctors that I was singing out loud.

Walking did help the scar tissue loosen up, keeping

blood clots from forming in my legs, and aided in faster healing and development of my new kidney. And I will tell you, I was feeling really good.

I stayed in the hospital only four days out of the seven expected. During this time, the drain tube was taken out, the catheter and ureter brace removed, and I urinated normally with the new organ. It was a great day when I was finally released to the hotel for my month-long recuperation.

While in the hotel, we met some great people, all at various stages of the kidney transplant process. Some were there for kidney transplant follow-up, some for initial workup to see if they could be an organ recipient, and yet others were getting their post-transplant checkup. My girlfriend and I developed a bond with these people, cheering each other on through physical battles and victories.

I checked into the hospital periodically, walked twice a day, and began to feel better and better. My medication was carefully noted and reduced until my healing rate ideally matched my medication allotment. Before we knew it, checkout time was upon us, and it was time to say goodbye to everyone. We checked out of our temporary hotel home, jumped into the car, went sightseeing for a few days, then headed back down south.

With God at my side, I fought this three-year war of waiting for my kidney. I battled against death by choosing to push through daily relentless pain, self-doubt, extreme lethargy, social reclusiveness, and rejection. Gout attacks in my joints, mind-twisting delirium, anemia, horrible headaches, haziness, lack of sleep, and so much more just added to my opportunities to rise above and persevere through faith in Jesus' name. I believed I was a conqueror, embracing every single second of my existence, regardless of what might have come and was recreated both inside and out by God.

Chapter 33:

RECORDS BROKEN

Not needing to get up at the crack of dawn for dialysis, I had the option to sleep in on Mondays, Wednesdays, and Fridays without being late to anything. No longer did a doctor have to remind me to do this or that, and I could eat anything I wanted to at any restaurant. Ice cream was not my enemy any longer, a dessert I would live on if it were humanly possible.

Before the transplant, I had built up to three hours of swimming laps in the pool, thirty miles of bike riding, and running nine and a half miles. Right after, it took everything in me to just walk a few miles around the neighborhood. I guessed that my body had to readjust to having a new organ doing its job.

When I told my nurses I was huffing and puffing around our neighborhood, they said that in the first three months, it would be tough to regain strength and be able to get back to where I was physically. I did not like this news one iota and defied it with everything in me.

Now that I had new "machinery" installed, I had a new physical lease on life and a lot of catching up to do. But as much as I wanted to run, I had to walk; metaphorically speaking. For the first three months, lifting nothing heavier than a gallon of milk was humbling and a little frustrating. Ok, a lot frustrating. I also could not drive for a while. As a man who loves road trips and driving, this was hard to accept. But sometimes the doctor knows best.

After a year of living and adjusting to my new miracle kidney, it was time to get my annual checkup. Because my doctors required me to have a chaperone for my first post-transplant checkup to make sure nothing happened during the recuperation time, Dad went with me. It was good to have him hang out on the road.

The seven-hour trip went by pretty quickly. We arrived in Iowa City that evening, checked into the hotel, and hit the hay. The next morning, we woke up and headed to the hospital for my blood work and yearly checkup.

I was pretty tired but ready to do whatever they needed. I weighed in, talked with my post-transplant nurse, another head nurse, the social worker, the dietician, my surgeon, and the pharmacist. We went over every aspect of my life from the time I had the transplant a year prior. After all of the interviews, it was time to do my physical fitness tests.

The first test was the hand grasp. This was a specialty exercise to see how strong one's grip was, indicating specific physical abilities and system strengths, muscle tone, endurance, strength, and nerve indicators. I grabbed a hold of the grip and squeezed as hard as I could. When I let go of it, I found out I beat my surgeon's grip score and set the record for the kidney transplant wing.

Next was the treadmill test to measure my heart rate and endurance. The nurse gave me instructions about the test, telling me it would incrementally increase in grade, getting steeper and steeper as time went by. This would increase my heart rate, breathing tempo, and gradually result in muscle fatigue. I was also told that the longest any transplant patient had walked on the treadmill was twenty minutes, set by a former Olympic runner a year prior.

After she told me that, it was on like Donkey Kong. I smiled at the nurse, climbed onto the treadmill, and she started the test. The speed and gradient were the same for a few minutes, and every two minutes the angle increased incrementally. Every ten minutes or so, the nurse asked how I was feeling, and I exuberantly told her I was doing awesome.

I kept walking as the platform belt angle kept increasing until, after an hour and fifteen minutes, I was swiftly walking at a gradient angle of forty degrees. I decided that my time and effort on the treadmill pretty much sealed the new record, so I stopped. Asking how I performed, the observation nurse said I had surpassed the Olympic runner's record by fifty-five minutes.

I was interested in seeing how long I could walk, and the record stuff was a bonus. She was speechless and could not believe what I had just done. To me, it was just another workout, but it nearly caused the nurse doing my treadmill test to miss her lunchtime. Go God.

From then on, people all over the hospital heard about my record on the treadmill. Nurses and doctors called me the "Legend." That was very humbling, to say the least.

To this day, I tell my post-transplant coordinator I hope what I did inspires others to push past their limits. I also tell them that God helped me set the record. You see, I stepped out and dared to do what was considered difficult at best and by faith surpassed everyone's expectations. It took about a year until everything fully healed, even more so than it was before my kidneys initially failed. My strength, endurance, and overall medical stability improved day to day. I truly felt like I had been given an entirely new body from my head to my feet, and there was no way but up.

Dr. Eric Shannon Parr

Chapter 34:

ACADEMIC FINISH LINE

I jumped back into long hours of relentless research shortly after returning home from my annual checkup. Having renewed physical and spiritual strength, propelling me towards my goal of becoming a doctor, nothing would stop me. Every day brought me closer and closer to defending my dissertation.

The last year and a half of holding ridiculously long hours day and night on my computer screen while doing dialysis and trying to survive affected my eyes, needing my prescription glasses adjusted a few times. I developed some pretty mean, dark circles under the eyes and some more gray hair, earning battle scars of what I fought for and overcame by the Grace of God.

Persevering over the next five months, I clawed, pushed, prayed, and believed my way through it all. It was a constant, never-ending breaking down and rebuilding of my academic mind. Much like the military, I had to know that I wanted it beyond anything else.

It was a journey of never settling for anything less than more and more physical, emotional, social, and academic thrashing. It was a destroying and stripping away of the old self, realizing the new, educated man, hoping to become a doctor at the other end of the academic pursuit.

After requesting from my Doctorate Board when and where I would present my doctoral defense, I received the approval. Finally, after years of sacrifice, I was set to either cross over to becoming a doctor or fail miserably. A few weeks later, I drove to the college, introduced myself as Eric Parr, and found the room set for my dissertation defense.

My Board members came into the room and grabbed their favorite coffee courtesy of yours truly. I greeted each of them with a self-assured "Welcome!" Energetically shaking their hands, I gave them handouts outlining and explaining my exhaustive dissertation research contents.

No more cramped fingers or knots in my back and shoulders from typing twelve hours straight in wooden coffee shop chairs. No more being mentally stressed constantly with deadlines. And finally, no more relentless dissertation Chair telling me to rewrite parts of my paper over and over, making it perfect.

In hindsight, I do not blame her. It was her job to stay on top of me, requiring new information every few days, seeing how I could make what was written scientifically effective, proactively structured, and theoretically supported. This intensive doctorate writing process was the hardest, most mentally challenging thing I had ever done in my life. Still is.

I hungered after the process of facing, embracing, and allowing this advanced academic process to recreate me. Many levels intellectually, including analytical processes, broadened mental capacity, and exhaustive knowledge of chosen research, played a crucial analytical part in my research. Study analysis and development of novel instrumentation were also created and included. Furthermore, discovery details and overall doctoral levels of academic perception and future performance implications were realized.

Never again would I experience the barrage of constant redirection and verbal hovering of my doctoral Chair. She was the master of breaking my academic will, seeing if I was committed to this whole doctor thing. Teetering on the edge of insanity, I had but one self-established, daily decision: choose to push through, do it to the best of my ability, or die.

Dressed in my doctoral best, I was ready to make a professional impression and seemed to do so based on how my Board responded when I walked in the room with confidence and determination in a kick-butt suit. I never wore a suit coat and tie during my entire doctorate program, and they liked it. Take advantage of every positive opportunity to gain an upper edge, I say.

I turned to my doctoral Defense board, consisting of top-revered doctors of the program, took a deep breath, and systematically delivered my dissertation defense. To defend and support my research, study, and ultimately my dissertation, I presented every single scientist, historical reference, applicable theoretical construct, novel research question, thematic element, and every peer-reviewed document within the last five years from that point in time. I explained how these and other parts mentioned came together flawlessly, with implication, and without doubt.

I showed how my discovery of the gap between facility managers' mandates and students' aesthetic requirements of classroom learning environments affects the well-being, academic achievement, and recruitment and retention of students. I displayed the implications and associated concentric effects of any given environment on an individual. As I was going through these and other parts of my dissertation defense, my Board seemed to be listening intently and with much interest. Of course, this might have been a good or bad sign.

I had better be perfect and thorough in every minute detail because at this level, I was expected to know the material inside and out, being THE expert in my chosen doctoral subject matter. If not, they would shred my work and make me start from scratch. With one casual statement and movement of the pen, it would all go away, nullifying everything I sacrificed for years to accomplish. Dr. Tim, the gentleman who was the executive director of the entire accelerated doctorate program and who allowed me back in during the time of my dialysis, was also on my Board.

After a forty-five-minute defense presentation, I asked for questions. I thanked everyone for attending, shut off the PowerPoint program, closed my computer, and waited in respectful silence for the verdict. I saw eyes dart back and forth across the room with exchanged, quiet utterances. Then it happened.

I was told my study was novel, unique, and revolutionary in my chosen doctoral field. I was further informed of the thoroughness and comprehensive interest in what my studies implied in the field of higher education and beyond. After their discussions, Dr. Tim stood up from his chair, walked around the desk, and directly up to me.

Quietly, and with absolute resolve, he cracked a smile, shook my hand, and said, "Congratulations, Dr. Eric Shannon Parr. I look forward to seeing what you will do with your amazing and truly novel research." That was the single most important collection of nouns and pronouns I had been waiting to hear for as long as I could remember. All the gut-busting work led me to this moment, and I was now a doctor of education with all of the rights, responsibilities, and privileges appointed unto me. I walked into that college as Eric Parr and out of it as Dr. Eric Shannon Parr, Ed.D. The most horrendously intensive process of my life was now complete.

I achieved a 4.0 GPA throughout my entire doctorate program. Because of this, I was invited to join the Intercollegiate National Honors Society Alpha Chi and the Golden Key International Honors Society. Receiving these scholarly acknowledgements and accolades was a true blessing from God for giving me supernatural academic abilities. He rewrote my past learning difficulties and failures when I chose to see what was possible by faith, helping me to take steps in realizing an incredible future.

Chapter 35:

THE JOURNEY CONTINUES

I would have never thought these words would come out of my mouth, much less be written on a page. But here ya go. I am now an educational research scientist, internationally published scientific author, theorist, and qualitative research expert whose scientific research boasts less than a one percent international research duplicity rate. My research theoretical framework is supported by the human ecological theory, implicated to generalize into virtually every form, function, and branch of science, technology, engineering, medicine, management, biodiversity, philosophy, military, and civilian adaptations of environmental influences, and others.

I possess expert knowledge in Kindergarten through grade twelve and college aesthetics, facility management practices and responsibilities, careers, and types.

Implications and theoretical applications include any student, instructor, and administrator directly or indirectly affected by, or included in the design, development, and implementation of any type of learning and training environment, virtual or otherwise. This includes any discipline, company, business, or practice anywhere in the world.

I am presently developing theories based on my research. I speak, lecture, consult, and write on scientific findings at businesses, schools, conferences, and special events. Textbooks and literature-based books are also in the works based on my scientific findings. Let me be clear, everything I have achieved and realized could not have been achieved without God through Jesus Christ. I walk daily through each step of my academic process with purpose, self-determined faith.

I speak about my explorations and experiences of going to Antarctica and Christchurch, New Zealand, and serving in the United States Navy. I share with college students the lessons I learned through the revelation of Jesus Christ. Being a former school counselor, I use the gifts and talents God has given to me to help those from all walks of life understand the strategies of overcoming even the smallest things.

I would not have had the courage, wisdom, or determination to see what could be possible unless I decided to step out and push through every obstacle when everyone and everything told me I could not succeed. Sometimes success looks exactly the way you think, such as my doctoral pursuit and its resultant favor, opportunities, and revelations. Still other times, it can take on different forms, allowing for growth and opportunity through the continued overcoming process, being flexible and adaptable. You never know what can be learned when great things are expected.

My kidney situation is great, although I am still immunosuppressed and will be for the rest of my life. This means my immune system performs at a very low rate due to medications, helping my body to continually realize my new kidney is not a foreign object that needs to be attacked and destroyed. For the same reasons, my old kidneys were left in when they were disconnected, helping my body think I still have the old kidneys.

They simply shriveled up, now just an internal souvenir from my miracle of life surgery. This practice of leaving the kidneys depends on the patient's presenting factors, including the type of disease, specific disorders of the organ, and comorbidity. In my case, it was a very normal procedure to do so.

Swimming in any untreated body of water because of bacteria or parasites is off limits. Biking and other outdoor activities are performed with caution. This has become a way of life for me now, and I have grown used to it over the years. Yes, it keeps me from doing some things I loved, but I have fun nonetheless.

I cannot hike through the back country where I encounter lakes, rivers, and streams, but I do what I have to do. Instead, I count my blessings and am forever thankful for what God did for me. The lie that I cannot go explore the outdoors is not something I entertain; I just need to be careful and take extra precautions when doing so.

I gained a very specific focus and clarity as to who I did and did not allow into my life during kidney dialysis, and carried this practice over to the present. Whether potential dates or friendships, I gauge them according to my health, professional pursuits, my spiritual belief system, and overall wants and needs. Since my transplant, I choose those that can support and promote positivity and forward-thinking momentum in every area of my life. My spiritual beliefs and discernment are a strong compass for developing long-lasting friendships, and I learned not to compromise my overall walk with God while choosing them.

When I became ill, many stopped being in my life, not being able to see me as a sick person. They were not willing or able to stick with me, showing me the truths beneath superficial actions and appearances. Sobering reality showed me what I truly needed and, most importantly, what kind of people I did not need, regardless of their social or professional status. One needs to look out for one's emotional, spiritual, and psychological health at all times.

My physical endurance went through the roof during that first year of healing, being able to run longer, breathe easier, and recuperate faster between workouts. I had no idea how much my body was stressed and limited physically because of the kidney disease. I was a pretty good athlete before, but how I now perform is beyond personal expectations. I can run for miles without having to catch my breath, swim forever in the pool, and ride my bike with little effort. I have also started weightlifting and powerlifting again.

Concerning my dietary needs, my kidneys continually get rid of all the poisons it builds up daily, not allowing my body to store wastes or high levels of minerals, fluids, and everything else that caused initial health-impeding reactions. Having no issues with side effects when eating the wrong thing, I can eat food like ice cream and steak without thinking of the ramifications, like the gout I suffered with for years. Of course, it is done with moderation. Most of the time I am good, other times, well, let me say I found a great pizza shop I should not be at so often.

I do not want to abuse the gift of life God has given to me and the miraculous way in which it happened. I did gain a little weight initially from the transplant because of all the things I could now eat, but I am acutely aware of keeping weight gain at bay. It is a daily choosing of life over death. Going on my ninth year as a very blessed kidney transplant survivor, I use my kidney dialysis and transplant experience to help others. I also speak, write, and advocate for kidney dialysis patients, organ donors and their families, and organ recipients at hospitals, dialysis centers, and special events.

I love to help others stay in the fight, never giving up. I am a strong advocate of overall fitness, a healthy lifestyle, and eating right. For those patients who will never be able to get a kidney replacement due to other health issues, I help them to find psychologically, socially, and spiritually healthy alternatives to shift their mindsets from what cannot be changed to what can be accomplished. And last but never least, I always share my faith and testimony of what God did and continues to do through His Son Jesus Christ in my life and what He wants to do in others' lives as well.

Despite all of the accomplishments and goals I have achieved, life continues to present challenges, limitations, and delays. As I have been updating this book, my father is fighting in the hospital. He is an incredibly tough man who has had his share of struggles and overcome much, with some of them having played into how he used to act towards his family. However, change has been apparent in his character, and I thank God for these transformations, regardless of how difficult or harrowing.

Resting in the knowledge of faith in my God through tangibly facing, embracing, and recreating impossibilities into unrealized destiny is the way I have chosen to live. This is the way I have learned to defy the lies of the apparent. DEFYING THE LIES is not a clever saying or catchy phrase, but what I believe with everything in me, reinforced with each overcome limit, struggle, and unforeseen circumstance through the supernatural power of Jesus Christ.

You see, we are all on this journey together, sharing more similarities than differences. We are all people fighting to survive in many ways, whether it is living off of machines, keeping the car running, or raising kids. Everyone is either trying to pass that driving test, survive eighth grade, going through a divorce, in a tough marriage, or even trying to love someone when they do not love you back.

Striving for a promotion at work, you work eighty hours a week in hopes that the boss will see your diligence. Maybe you suffer from residual emotional hurts from church issues or feel judged by your singles group. Perhaps attempting to kick bad habits is a never-ending failure, or you have been in and out of rehab with the same addictive results.

You might even be dealing with constant abuse and rejection at home and school. Giving up on yourself, you plead, pray, and beg that it would all stop, or you will make it stop anyway you can. Being a military veteran, you could be dealing with a whole host of medical or mental issues that never seem to go away, because the places veterans go for help miss the mark.

If you can relate to one issue or another, maybe many of them, then this book was for you, and I am happy you chose to read it. It does not get any easier, but there is a better way to deal with them using the incident for growth and transformation.

Now it is time for you to readily decide. Will you stop making all kinds of excuses for yourself, blaming everything from here to kingdom come on your circumstances, your past, limitations, or those around you? Are you ready to stop believing the always available lies that you cannot overcome your downfalls or setbacks?

If not, then you will always be right where you are. But if you decide to seek what is not seen, receive what has not yet been given, and realize what has not been proposed, then I congratulate you on an incredible start to an unbelievable destiny!

Just ask Jesus into your heart and ask for forgiveness of your sins, as it says in John 3:16. He will redeem you and instill strength through faith to begin overcoming any issue. I guarantee you it will be the start of your transformative journey with God to learn, grow, and heal. You will begin to see answers, strategies, and possibilities materialize in even the smallest areas of struggle, empowering you to stand strong through anycircumstance with God. Pray this prayer to begin your transformative journey:

Get ready for your present and especially your future to be supernaturally recreated! The decision you have made will inevitably steer you on a course of fantastic revelation and untapped faith never before seen. Before you know it, you will begin to see things in a whole new light, and perceptions of defeat and hopelessness will begin to disappear. Things will begin to change in even the smallest details, from personal, professional, physical, and every other area of your life, according to the plans God has already set in motion. Seeking God will reveal your perfectly created future, learning about yourself, evolving along the way.

You are more!

Dr. Eric Shannon Parr

Made in the USA
Monee, IL
01 September 2025